CHROMATIC**LEAD**
GUITARTECHNIQUES

Discover Approach Notes, Enclosures, Delayed Resolution & Other Chromatic Concepts

SHAUN**BAXTER**

FUNDAMENTAL**CHANGES**

Chromatic Lead Guitar Techniques

Discover Approach Notes, Enclosures, Delayed Resolution & Other Chromatic Concepts

ISBN: 978-1-78933-421-0

Published by **www.fundamental-changes.com**

Copyright © 2023 Shaun Baxter

Edited by Joseph Alexander

For over 350 Free Guitar Lessons with Videos Check Out

www.fundamental-changes.com

Join our free Facebook Community of Cool Musicians

www.facebook.com/groups/fundamentalguitar

Tag us for a share on Instagram: **FundamentalChanges**

Cover Image Copyright: Shutterstock, Ching Design47

All A7 CAGED lines recorded and mixed at W.M. Studios by Phil Hilborne.

All solo studies recorded and mixed at Brakenhurst Studio by Shaun Baxter.

All transcriptions by Shaun Baxter

Contents

About the Author

Shaun Baxter is a world-renowned guitar player and the UK's most experienced and respected rock guitar teacher.

He was a founder member of The Guitar Institute in London in 1986 (which was partnered with the London College of Music and became the biggest trade school for guitar in Europe), where he taught every week for over twenty years. He went on to be Head of Guitar at Guitar-X in London before, in 2003, becoming an owner and the Academic Director of The Academy of Music and Sound (AMS), a national network of musical schools, opening centres in Exeter, Southampton, Swindon, Aylesbury, Hitchin, Gateshead, Birmingham, Edinburgh and Glasgow. At one point, via their various apprenticeship schemes, AMS were the biggest employer in the Scottish music industry and whose alumni includes Lewis Capaldi.

Shaun composed the world's first Grade 8 Guitar syllabus for Trinity College, wrote the UK's National Operational Standards (NOS) for music performance, and contributed to magazines such as *The Guitar Magazine, Guitar World, Metal Hammer* and *Guitar Techniques* (for whom he wrote a popular and influential column every month for 27 years).

Through his teaching, Shaun helped to pioneer popular music education in the UK and taught many prominent guitar players and teachers, such as Rick Graham, Andy James, Jon Gomm and Justin Sandercoe, as well as many others who have found fame in the music industry with artists such as Public Image Ltd, Asia, Craig David, Moby, Wynton Marsalis, Haken, Martin Taylor, Steve Hackett, Rick Wakeman, Mike Oldfield, The Art of Noise, Leo Sayer, Pet Shop Boys, Roger Waters and Queen.

During the '90s, Shaun was a member of the Composition Department at the London College of Music and also lectured at Brunel University, Leeds College of Music, University of West London, Bath Spa University, Coventry University and Rostock University of Music and Drama (East Germany).

In 1993 Shaun recorded his ground-breaking *Jazz Metal* solo album. He has performed with players such as Uli Jon Roth (Scorpions), Neil Murray (Whitesnake, Black Sabbath) and Ron "Bumblefoot" Thal (Guns & Roses), and also toured the world and/or recorded with artists such as Princess, John Sloman (Gary Moore/ Uriah Heep), Todd Rundgren and Carl Palmer of Emerson Lake and Palmer.

"He is one of the greatest musicians I have played with."

– Carl Palmer, legendary progressive rock drummer

As an artist, Shaun has been an official endorsee of Marshall Amplification, Cornford Amplification, Fender Guitars, Patrick Eggle Guitars, Line 6 effects, Two-Note Audio Engineering, and Picato Strings.

Finally, Shaun was one of only 8 heavy metal guitar players (along with Edward Van Halen, Joe Satriani, Steve Vai, Yngwie Malmsteen, Nuno Bettencourt, Michael Schenker and Paul Gilbert) featured in the world's biggest-selling music book, *Guitar: A Complete Guide for the Player* (2002). He appeared in a list of "The top 50 rock guitar players since the 1980s" in an article which appeared in *Guitarist* magazine, and was also included in *The Guitarist Book of Guitar Players* (1994), which details "the world's most influential guitarists and bass players", in which Jazz Metal topped its 50 recommended fusion guitar recordings.

Introduction

Chromatic notes are *non-scale* notes. The word *chroma* is the Greek word for colour, and chromatic notes are a great way of making your lines sound more ear-catching.

Whether thinking in terms of painting pictures or creating flavours, chromatic notes will add colour and spice to your playing by offering you nearly twice as many notes to choose from (compared to a "normal" seven-note scale). Crucially, they give us the opportunity to add tension (dissonance) then release it (consonance), rather than just dwelling on "safe" scale notes all the time.

For the purposes of this book, we will view each chromatic note as a form of tension that will be resolved to a scale note (usually a chord-tone) either a half step above or below the chromatic note.

The study of chromatic approaches will be divided into the following chapters:

- **Chromatic Approach Notes**

- **Chromatic Bridging**

- **Chromatic Enclosures**

- **Delayed Resolution**

- **12-tone Rows**

- **Mixed Chromatic Techniques**

Each chromatic concept can be fully understood by studying its application to a single scale and we will learn each technique around the A Mixolydian scale, before applying the same concepts to Mixolydian in different keys.

Once you have worked your way through the examples in this book, you will be able to apply the same concepts to any other scale.

The first four chapters all follow the same structure. First you will learn useful lines based around each concept in all five shapes of the Mixolydian scale using the CAGED system, before learning a solo study that challenges you to play them in different keys.

The final two chapters are devoted to solo studies that combine all the chromatic concepts and will reinforce your skills.

Line Examples

Lines, Not Exercises

Chromaticism works best when it strikes a balance between other musical elements. So, instead of simply playing boring, repetitive exercises, we are going to focus on learning well-balanced, musical lines from the start. These will serve as practical templates and provide inspiration when creating your own musical vocabulary.

Line Distribution

Like any set of scale patterns, each shape provides unique physical opportunities to play musical ideas that fit comfortably around your fingers. For this reason, it makes sense to learn different licks for each shape. By doing this, simply moving to a new position on the neck will unlock a whole new vocabulary and help you to keep playing fresh ideas as you move from one area of the neck to another.

Other Scales

Although chromatic techniques are only applied to the Mixolydian scale in the various musical examples, many of those examples will see the Mixolydian being flanked by other commonly-used scales from the same root note. These scales will be indicated in the accompanying analysis, as and when they occur.

Solo Studies

Each solo study is crammed with CAGED Mixolydian lines that use the various chromatic concepts studied. Each one involves transposing Mixolydian through the keys of A7, C7, D7, F7 and G7. Each solo contains four bars of each chord and you will learn to move from A Mixolydian to C Mixolydian to D Mixolydian etc, as the solo progresses.

I've included fast and slow backing tracks in the audio download to help you learn and practice these solos

Transposing the A Scales

Before studying the solos, you should practise transposing each of the A Mixolydian CAGED shapes presented in this book to other keys (especially C7, D7, F7 and G7).

The main thing is to focus on the root note within each shape and shift it accordingly to relocate the whole pattern to the appropriate area of the fretboard.

For **C7**, shift any A Mixolydian Shape **up 3 frets** or **down 9 frets**

For **D7**, shift any A Mixolydian Shape **up 5 frets** or **down 7 frets**

For **F7**, shift any A Mixolydian Shape **up 8 frets** or **down 4 frets**

For **G7**, shift any A Mixolydian Shape **up 10 frets** or **down 2 frets**

Context

It's important to visualise each scale shape when working through the musical examples, so that you don't get lost and struggle to apply what you've learned to other musical contexts. Although it may be slow going at first, make sure you remain aware of how every note you play relates to a particular scale shape and its intervals.

To reinforce the concept of adapting and reapplying information, many of the solo studies feature A7 CAGED lines taken from earlier in that chapter, often transposed from A7 to fit one of the other four dominant 7 chords.

To help you analyse these lines, every example in this book has been annotated. All chromatic notes are indicated by an asterisk so that you can distinguish them from the notes that belong to the Mixolydian scale if you can't already hear them!

Each chromatic technique is indicated by the following abbreviations:

A.N. = Approach Note

Br. = Bridging

Enc. = Enclosure

Del. Res. = Delayed Resolution

Musical Anticipation

Although most of notes in each four-bar section relate to the underlying chord, the notes at the end of the final bar in each four-bar section often relate to the chord in the subsequent bar. This is because *anticipating chord changes* is a commonly-used technique, which helps to give a sense of forward movement to your playing. Any tension set up at the end of a bar will be resolved upon the arrival of the new chord.

Technical Options and Consideration

Chromatic notes are not confined to a single style, although they are more appropriate to some genres than others. I chose a Country Rock style for this book as it represents a convenient half-way house between Jazz and Rock. This often led me to use hybrid picking (a mixture of pick and fingers of the picking hand) and this technique is notated in the transcription. However, you are not obliged to stick to this and you should be aware that chromatic ideas can be applied to a whole host of extended techniques, such as right-hand tapping etc, so I encourage you to experiment in your favoured style.

One aspect of Country Rock that provides an additional twist is where chromatic movements occur across two adjacent strings or incorporate open strings. This happens throughout the various solo studies and you should pay attention to how this sounds.

Country Rock players love open strings because it allows them to mimic pedal-steel effects. However, this does mean that much of that vocabulary is key-specific. This generally doesn't bother most Country guitarists because they often play in *open* keys like E or A.

Depending on the genre of music you play, you will need to decide whether an open string line is portable or not. If you are a Jazz player, for example, you will probably want to develop a repertoire of lines that can be transposed to any key without the need for modification.

Adapting to Tempo

Playing techniques are often adjusted unconsciously as the tempo changes. For example, you may use more hammer-ons and pull-offs at high tempos, but pick more at slower tempos.

Similarly, depending on the amount of gain you like to use, you may end up adding some palm muting to clean things up. So, although I have faithfully transcribed what I played in each musical example, I have not been so pedantic as to indicate where a slight amount of palm muting has been used. Use your ears to detect this and adjust accordingly!

Get the Audio

The audio files for this book are available to download for free from **www.fundamental-changes.com**. The link is in the top right-hand corner. Click "Download Audio" and choose your instrument. Select the title of this book from the menu, and complete the form to get your audio.

We recommend that you download the files directly to your computer (not to your tablet or phone) and extract them there before adding them to your media library. If you encounter any difficulty, we provide technical support within 24 hours via the contact form.

For over 350 free guitar lessons with videos check out:

www.fundamental-changes.com

Join our free Facebook Community of Cool Musicians

www.facebook.com/groups/fundamentalguitar

Tag us for a share on Instagram: **FundamentalChanges**

Chapter One: Chromatic Approach Notes

A *chromatic approach note* is any non-scale note added to a melody which resolves to a scale note from either a semitone (half step) above or below.

Once you play a chromatic note, you need to learn how to resolve the tension it creates by targeting a scale note (often a chord tone). Applying chromaticism with control will help you to avoid descending into tuneless chaos, and the easiest place to start is to explore the simplest chromatic technique: *approach notes*. This is how they work:

Imagine you play four notes from an A7 arpeggio (A, C#, E, G):

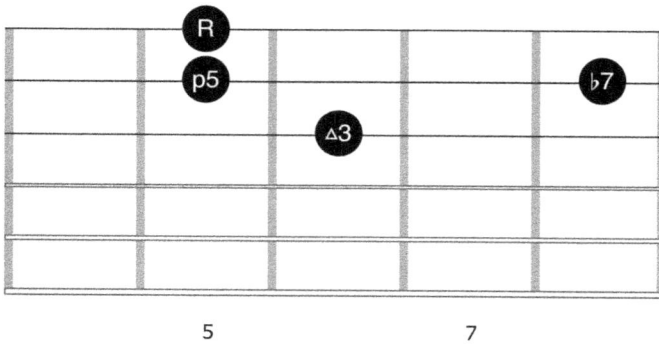

Let's add a chromatic approach note (Eb) a semitone below the E natural. The Eb is played on an off-beat (the "and" of beat 1) to land on the target E note on beat two. Play the 4th fret with your first finger and slide into the 5th fret target note.

Figure 1

Here's the same A7 arpeggio fragment. This time we approach the A note from a semitone above (Bb). Adding a chromatic approach note a semitone above has a more dissonant effect than one a semitone below. Again, the chromatic note is played on an off-beat to land on the target on beat 3.

Figure 2

In Jazz, there is a whole science surrounding whether a chromatic note is played on an off-beat (the most palatable option) or a down-beat (the most dissonant one), so when you're learning these examples make sure you observe where the chromatic note is placed and the effect it creates.

Note length is something to be aware of. The longer you linger on a chromatic note, the more it will prolong the dissonance for the listener. Conversely, the quicker you play it, the more liberties can be taken, as any tension will be brief.

In the next section you will learn to introduce chromatic approach notes around the five shapes of the A Mixolydian scale.

A Note About the Audio and Notation

All the examples for this book were recorded at 208bpm with the snare on beats two and four, which is standard for Country Rock.

You might feel that the rhythms are phrased as 1/16th notes at 104bpm, but they are actually very fast 1/8th notes at 208bpm and the notation is correct.

The count-ins are all in half time (104bpm) so that the track doesn't feel too frantic. If you're struggling to find the pulse, listen to the hi-hats!

A Mixolydian Scale Reference Diagrams

The section overleaf provides a quick reference for all five shapes of the A Mixolydian scale in the CAGED system. You can flip back there to refresh your memory on the shapes but I will point out which shape(s) are being used to create musical lines as we go.

Shape 1

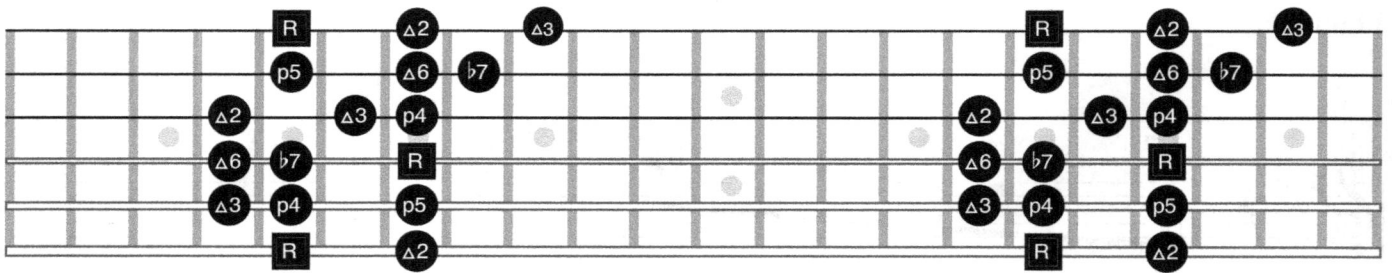

Shape 2

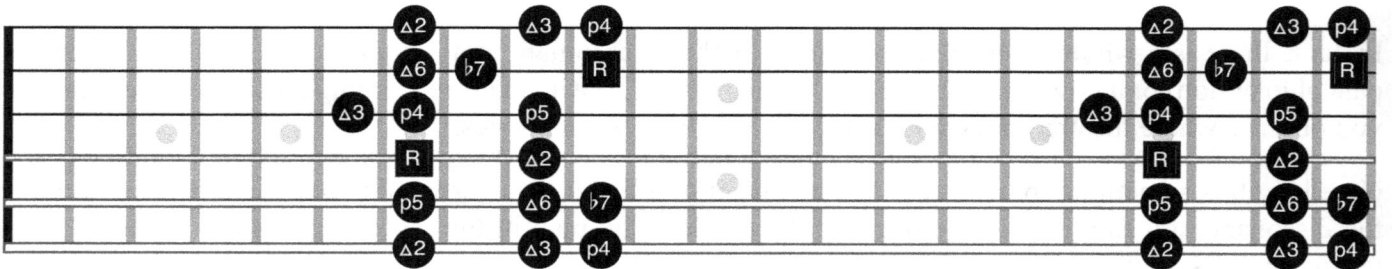

Shape 3

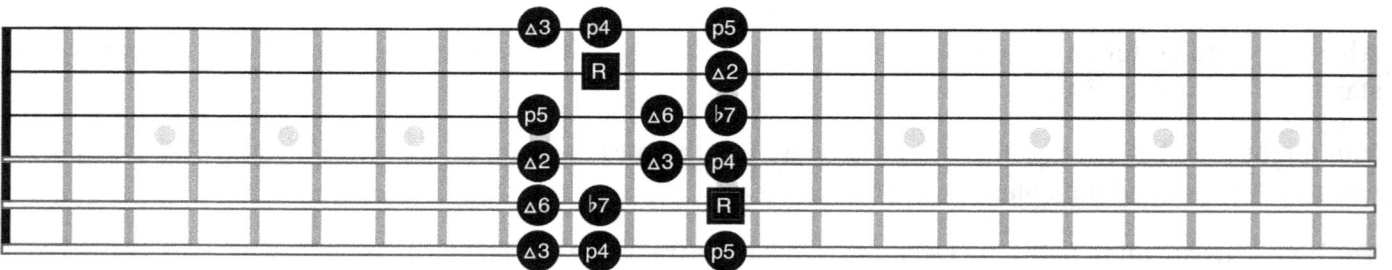

Shape 4

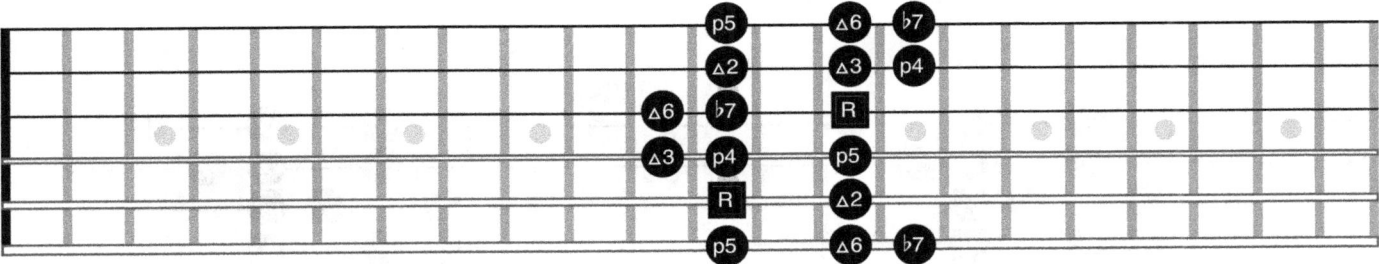

Shape 5

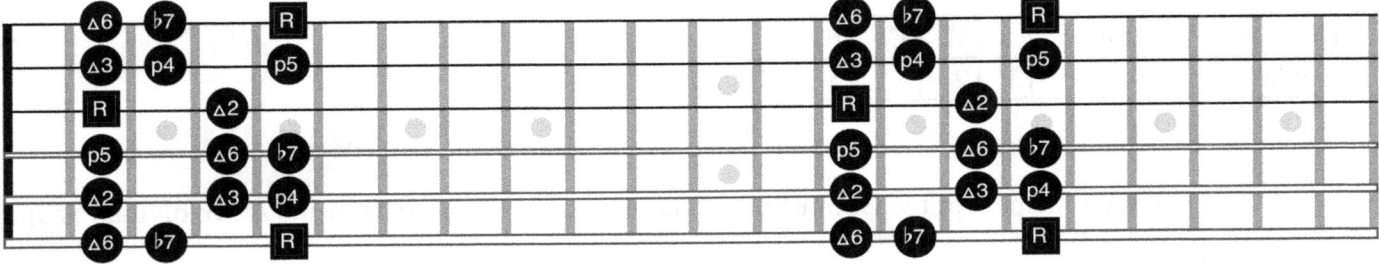

A7 CAGED Lines Featuring Chromatic Approach Notes

We'll begin in Shape 1 of A Mixolydian. The complete scale shape is shown here, with the root note on the sixth string at the 5th and 17th frets.

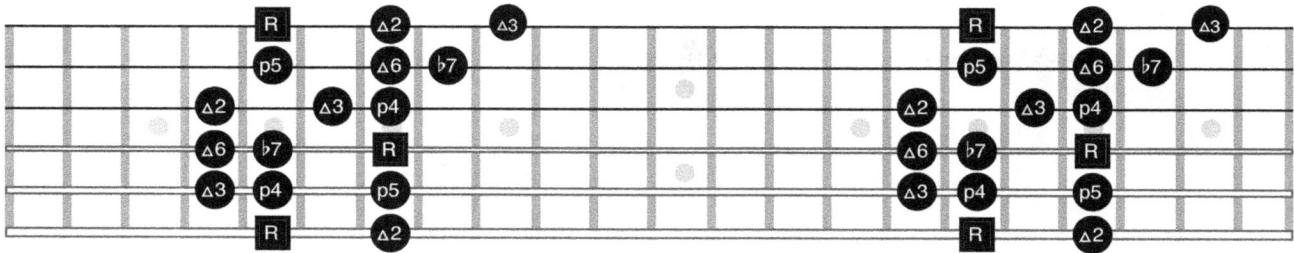

From the A Mixolydian scale we can extract the five-note Dominant Pentatonic scale.

A Dominant Pentatonic	A	B	C#	E	G
Formula	1	2	3	5	b7

Example 1a is based on Shape 1 of the Dominant Pentatonic scale, which exists inside A Mixolydian Shape 1.

A Dominant Pentatonic Shape 1

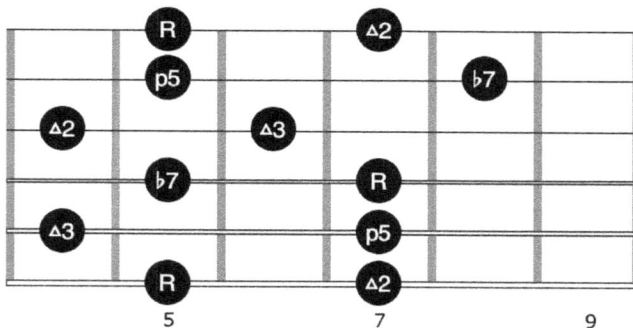

In this line I descend in a succession of 6-note groupings, with the first note of each group approached by a chromatic note a half step below. Notice that each chromatic note is played on a down-beat.

Example 1a

In the next example, each chromatic note is played on an off-beat, so it won't stick out as prominently.

This line begins in Shape 1, then combines A Mixolydian CAGED shapes to travel along the length of the neck. Each four-note motif starts with the lowest note of a 3rd interval, then approaches the highest note of that 3rd from a half step below before returning to the lowest note.

Example 1b

The chromatic notes in the next example also approach scale notes from below. However, now there are a mix of rhythmic approaches and the chromatic notes are played on both on-beats and off-beats.

The line combines shapes 1 and 2 and finishes in bar four with a Hendrix-style A Minor Pentatonic idea. Scales with a minor third are often used against dominant chords in order to add some bluesy grit. Here the minor third (C) of A Minor Pentatonic clashes with the happier-sounding major third in the chord and the Mixolydian scale's C#.

Example 1c

Example 1d combines on- and off-beat chromatic approach notes. Bar two drifts from A Mixolydian to A Minor Pentatonic and back to Mixolydian in bar three. It is based entirely around the notes of an A major triad (A C# E). The three-note groupings create an engaging "3 over 4" feel.

Example 1d

In Example 1e, I play more on- and off-beat chromatic approach notes from a half step below each target note. However, I now introduce a chromatic approach note from a half step *above* the target (the fourth note of bar three). Chromatic approach notes from above generally sound more dissonant than those from below.

Example 1e

All the chromatic approach notes in the following line are played from above and on the off-beat.

Example 1f

The final example rooted in Shape 1 features an equal mix of on- and off-beat chromatic notes, approaching both from above and below. Again, note the bluesy A Minor Pentatonic ending.

Example 1g

Now we shift up the neck to learn some lines based around A Mixolydian Shape 2.

We've learned that chromatic notes played on down-beats are more dissonant that those played on off-beats, but here we're taking the dissonance a step further by playing each chromatic note twice.

This line was inspired by Dixie clarinettist Jerry Fuller on a recording with Louis Armstrong and I'm sure you will agree that the effects are quite striking.

The idea finishes off with an A Minor 6 Pentatonic scale beginning from the second half of bar five. (The minor 6 pentatonic scale is similar to the minor pentatonic, but has the formula 1 b3 4 5 6 rather than 1 b3 4 5 b7).

Example 1h

In this example, I only use approach notes from a half step above. Each one is played on the off-beat.

Example 1i

Example 1j is the first of three examples using A Mixolydian Shape 3 and combines a mix of approaches.

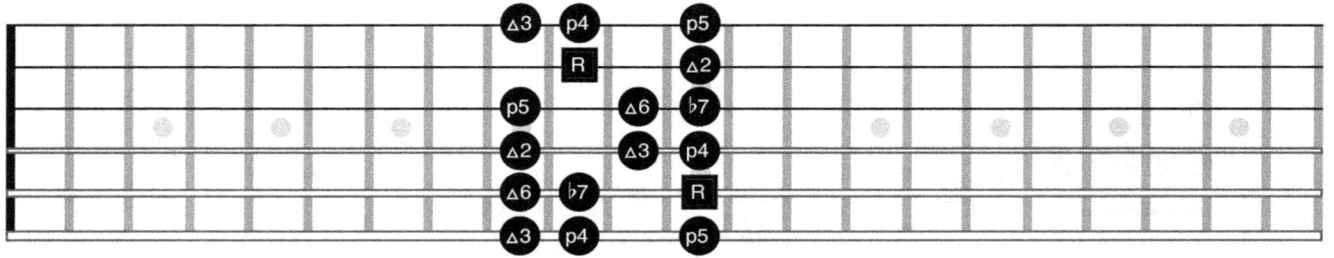

The first two bars of this line include chromatic approach notes from a half step below each target note. Each chromatic note is on the off-beat and all the target notes are from the tonic A Major triad.

In bars 4-5, there is a succession of four-note, 3rd interval motifs, where the lowest note of each side-steps to another note a half step below before returning. The fourth note is a diatonic 3rd above the first.

The final note in bar five is chromatic and resolves a half step down to the first note in bar six, which features approach notes from below. It concludes with an A Minor 6 Pentatonic scale idea in bar seven.

Example 1j

The next lick also begins by targeting an A Major triad. Each beat starts with a chromatic approach note a half step below the target note. In bars 3-4, we ascend an A7 arpeggio with each note side-stepping back and forth from a note a half step below. Again, notice the 3 over 4 feel created by playing three-note groupings in even 1/8th notes.

Example 1k

The final Shape 3 example is based around diatonic triads and highlights a mix of approaches. In the first two bars, I use a chromatic approach note to introduce the triad in the second half of each bar. Bar three then features a chromatic note played from a half step above.

Example 11

The following examples are built around A Mixolydian Shape 4.

The first example contains diatonic triads that descend through the scale. I play all the approach notes on a down-beat from a half step below, apart from the one at the end of bar five. Although they are a half step below the target note, the first note of bar one, and the fifth notes of bars two and four, are not shown with an asterisk because they are not chromatic and are scale notes of A Mixolydian.

Example 1m

A7

The following line demonstrates the same concept, but this time the diatonic triads ascend through the scale.

Example 1n

Next, I use chromatic notes a half step below with a mixture of on- and off-beat approaches.

Example 1o

The final Shape 4 idea features a mix of on- and off-beat chromatic notes approaching target notes from both a half step above and below. All the target notes are in the tonic A Major triad.

Example 1p

Next, we shift up to the first of two examples in A Mixolydian Shape 5.

In the first two bars I play a succession of descending diatonic triads (E, D, C and Bm). In each four-note motif, an on-beat chromatic note approaches the lowest note in each triad from a half step below.

Example 1q

The final example features a healthy mix of on- and off-beat chromatic approach notes from both a half step above and below A Major chord tones (and also to a B note in bar four). It begins in Shape 5 but ends up in Shape 1.

Example 1r

In the next section, you will learn a longer piece I've written that combines all these elements into a musical solo study. As with all the studies, it moves through the key centres of A7, C7, D7, F7 and G7, with four bars on each. This means that every four bars you'll be changing key to a different Mixolydian scale.

Sometimes, you'll stay in the same position on the neck but use a different shape when the key changes, and sometimes you'll simply move the current shape up the guitar neck, just like a barre chord. Either way, treat this as an opportunity to get the sound of these approach note patterns into your fingers and ears in a musical setting.

Chromatic Approach Notes Solo Study Analysis

Here is a breakdown of the ideas used in the solo study.

Bars 1-4

A minor 3rd is one of the most commonly added chromatic notes to Mixolydian. Here, I use it in a double-stop idea reminiscent of Chuck Berry. Notice how the repeated five-note grouping adds rhythmic interest and how we shift to C Mixolydian two notes early in anticipation of the C7 in bar five.

Bars 5-8

This section features Example 1e transposed to C7. Most of the chromatic notes are used to approach C Major chord tones. However, the second chromatic note in bar seven approaches the note D from a half step above.

Bars 9-12

This Brent Mason-style line uses open strings (a common feature of Country Rock) to create an open, resonant, banjo-influenced sound. Bar Eleven contains an approach note that I bend up a half step to the target note for a slinkier form of expression

Bars 13-16

In this section, I play Example 1p transposed to F7. Every chromatic note in this passage is used to approach a chord tone of F7 from a half step below or above.

Bars 17-20

A b3 is added in both octaves throughout this Albert Lee-influenced line. Again, the banjo-style sustained notes and open strings allow all my notes to ring into each other for a bit of dissonance. This is the first time a chromatic note approaches another on an adjacent string.

Bars 21-24

There are no chromatic notes used in this Albert Lee-style double-stop line, but it does help me to create a well-balanced solo. Here, pure Mixolydian offers a temporary respite from the ear-twisting dissonance of chromaticism.

Bars 25-28

The lick from Example 1l is used here, albeit transposed to C7 and with a modified ending. Bars 25-26 incorporate chromatic notes with diatonic triads. Try to identify which ones are used.

Bars 29-32

I kick off this section with a bluesy open string D Minor Pentatonic idea. There are more sustained notes in the bluegrass-influenced ideas that follow it in bars 30-32.

Bars 33-36

These bars feature a variation on the Albert Lee-style double-stop and open string approach used earlier. I anticipate the G7 in bar thirty-seven by a few beats by using the last two double-stops to create a *perfect cadence* of D7 to G.

Bars 37-40

As in bars 17-20, this section includes chromatic approaches from an adjacent string that I allow to ring together to produce a Country Rock feel. The final three notes of bar forty anticipate the A7 in the following bar.

Bars 41-48

I begin with the first four bars from Example 1j played with more picking due to the slower tempo.

Bars 38-39 include approach notes from a half step below a two-octave A Major triad, whereas bars 43-44 take a more linear approach based on diatonic thirds. This theme is continued in C Mixolydian over the following C7 chord.

Bars 49-52

At the start of bar forty-nine, I use the b3 (F natural) to approach the 2nd (E natural) from a half step above. At the end of the same bar, another F natural (b3) an octave lower on the G string is used to approach the F# (3rd) at the start of bar fifty. Finally, the F note at the end of bar fifty-two is played in anticipation, and is part of the phrase for, the F7 in bar fifty-three.

Bars 53-56

This section uses Example 1f transposed to F7 where I focus on approaching various chord tones of F7 (F A C Eb) chromatically from above. The final four notes of bar fifty-six are taken from F Minor Pentatonic.

Bars 57-60

This section comprises a transposed and modified version of Example 1n. Each bar contains a series of ascending three-note diatonic triads (G, Am, B°, C, Dm, Em and F) approached from a half step below.

Bars 61-64

This Johnny Hiland-influenced section begins with a repeated six-note grouping before continuing with double-stops on the G and B strings, and slides up the A string.

Bars 65-68

To add a bit of light and shade, the first four notes of bar sixty-six are from C Minor 6 Pentatonic scale before switching to the brighter sounding C Major Blues scale.

C Minor 6 Pentatonic	C	Eb	F	G	A
Formula	1	b3	4	5	6

C Major Blues	C	D	Eb	E	G	A
Formula	1	2	b3	3	5	6

The last note of bar sixty-eight is D, which I use to anticipate the D7 in the following bar.

Bars 69-72

This section is a modified version of Example 1m transposed to F7 and relocated from Shape 4 to Shape 1. It is formed from a series of descending diatonic triads, each approached from a note a half step below.

Bars 73-76

Here, I use Example 1r transposed to F7, which includes a balanced mix of half step approaches from above and below. Other than the start of bar seventy-six, chord tones are targeted throughout.

Bars 77-80

I conclude by returning to some Merle Travis-influenced open string banjo rolls. Bar seventy-seven uses the notes of G Dorian, a common substitution for G Mixolydian, to create a bluesier sound. Bar seventy-eight sees a return to G Mixolydian and every chromatic note is used to approach a chord tone of G (G, B or D) from a half step below on an adjacent string.

G Dorian	G	A	Bb	C	D	E	F
Formula	1	2	b3	4	5	6	b7

You'll find fast and slow backing tracks for the study pieces in the audio download bundle.

CHROMATIC APPROACH-NOTES SOLO STUDY

[Each chromatic note is indicated with an asterisk]

A.N. = approach-note movement

(Shaun Baxter)

G7
Let ring throughout
A.N.
A7
Ring
BU
C7
D7
Let ring throughout
1/4 (curl)
A.N.

F7
33
34
35
36
Hold
BU
PB8
PB8
PB8
LD
A.N.
G7
37
38
39
40
Let ring throughout
A7
41
42
43
44
C7
45
46
47
48

D7
Let ring throughout
A.N.
F7
A.N.
(1/4 curl)
G7
A.N.
Let ring throughout
A7
(6)
A.N.

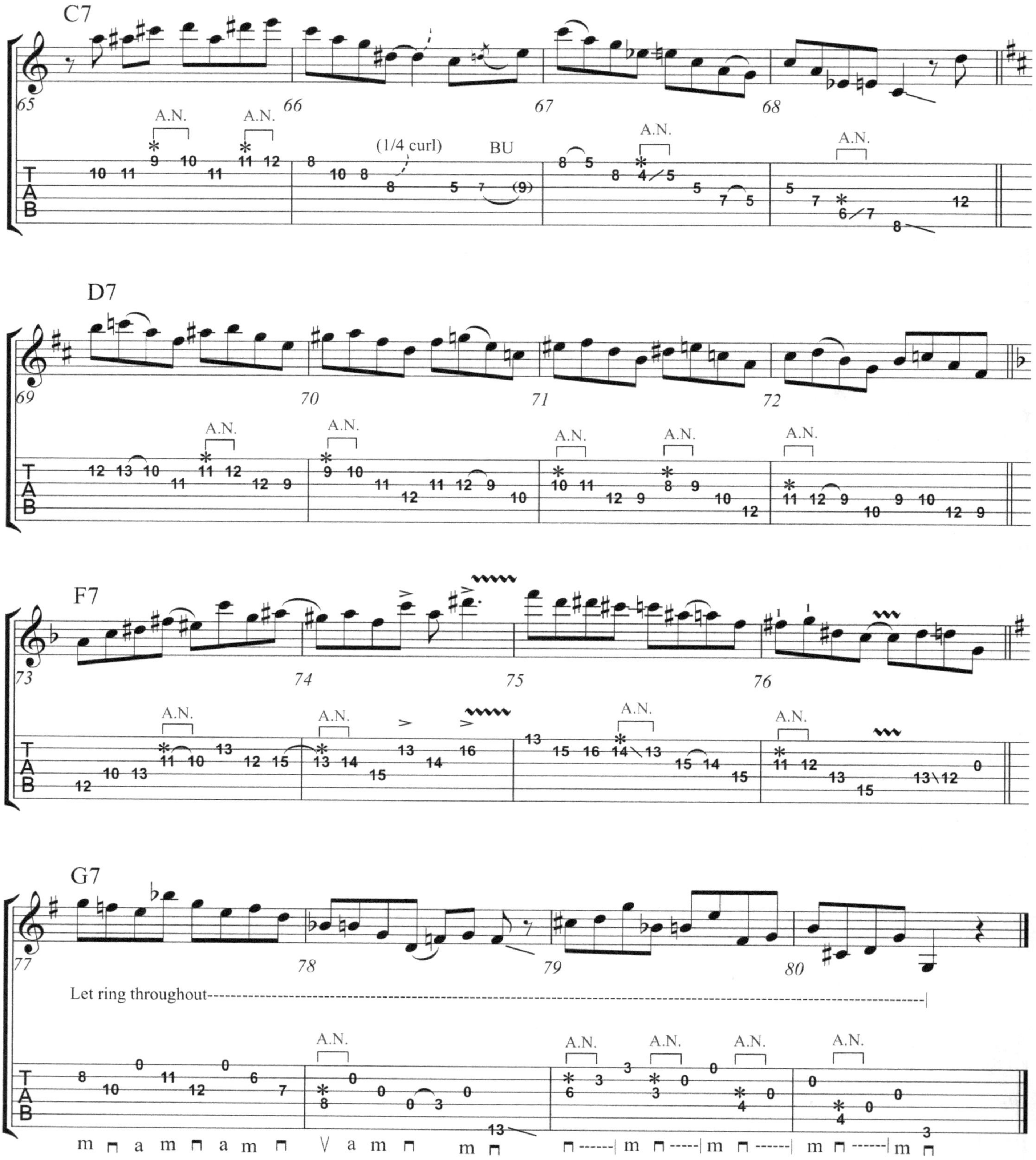
C7
A.N.
(1/4 curl)
BU
D7
F7
G7
Let ring throughout
TAB

Chapter Two: Chromatic Bridging

Chromatic Bridging is the practice of using one or more consecutive chromatic notes to link one scale note with another. In its simplest form, this is when a chromatic note is used to link two notes a whole tone apart. For example, the note B could be linked to the note A via Bb.

Figure 3

But it's also possible to take two notes much further apart and simply fill all the gaps in between. For example, if descending from the note B to the note G, we could play B, Bb, A, Ab, G.

Figure 4

A7 CAGED Lines Featuring Chromatic Bridging

All the examples in this chapter show how chromatic bridging can be used in conjunction with the chromatic approach notes from the previous chapter to create new vocabulary in each of the Mixolydian CAGED shapes.

We start with the first in a series of lines stemming from A Mixolydian Shape 1.

Jazz, a style that frequently uses chromatic notes, has explored the effect created when notes are placed either on or off the beat. This led to the formalisation of the Mixolydian Bebop scale, which contains eight notes instead of seven, and has a built-in approach note. It is simply the Mixolydian scale with an added major seventh interval.

A Bebop Scale	A	B	C#	D	E	F#	G	G#
Formula	1	2	3	4	5	6	b7	7

A Bebop Scale Shape 1

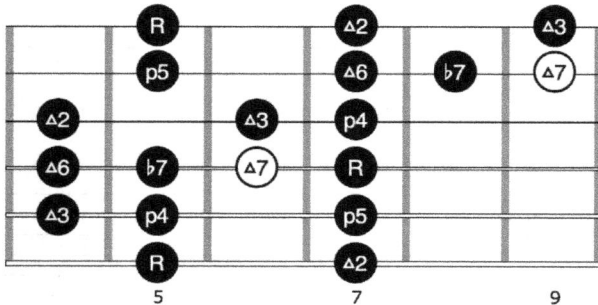

The extra natural 7th scale degree (G#) is used as a passing note that ensures all the chord tones (A C# E and G) land on the down-beat when playing the scale stepwise.

1	*and*	2	*and*	3	*and*	4	*and*	1
A	B	C#	D	E	F#	G	G#	A

The G# creates a natural chromatic *bridge* between G and A and is shown in two different octaves below.

Example 2a

The next line also uses the A Bebop scale in Shape 1, this time ascending.

The Bebop scale allows you to begin a scale line from any chord tone and still cause all the other chord tones to land on a down-beat as you ascend or descend the scale in straight 1/8th or 1/16th notes.

Example 2b

The principle of using a chromatic note to bridge two notes a tone apart is extended in Example 2c by looking at other tone-wide gaps within the Mixolydian, and starts with a whole succession of chromatic bridges.

It is also possible to think of this line as the note A linked chromatically to C#, followed by C# linked chromatically (descending) to G. Try to stay conscious of which scale intervals are being linked by chromatic notes throughout each example.

Example 2c

This line was inspired by the saxophonist David Sanborn, and although the second half of bar one could be viewed in terms of approach notes, it can also be seen as a C (b3 of A Minor Pentatonic) linked chromatically ascending to an E. It features a balanced blend of bridging and a simple approach note movement in bar three.

Example 2d

Now let's take these principles to A Mixolydian Shape 2. The following Pat Martino-style line also features a mixture of bridging and single approach notes.

Example 2e

Let's move up to Shape 3 and learn a line that shifts laterally along the length of the neck.

The theme in the first two bars is a descending series of diatonic triads (A, G, F# and Em), each with an approach note. Again, there is a mix of bridging and single approach notes. Every note is targeted by a chromatic note from a half step below.

Example 2f

Example 2g starts in Shape 3 and transitions down into Shape 2. It kicks off with a large ascending bridging movement linking the note B to E.

The other two chromatic bridges have a descending motion that links two notes a tone apart. As in Example 2b, we switch to the A Minor 6 Pentatonic in bar four for a bluesy effect.

Example 2g

This Charlie Parker-influenced idea starts off with two ascending bridging movements that link notes a tone apart before finishing with a large descending chromatic bridge between C# and A.

Example 2h

The next lick features tight chromatic interplay and bridging motions. The first four bridges link notes a tone apart. The fifth links B to G, and the sixth (in bar five) shows a chromatic bridge used between the b3 (C) and 4th (D) of A Minor Pentatonic.

The C# note is shown with an asterisk in bar five because it's used as a chromatic bridge between the C and D of A Minor Pentatonic.

Example 2i

Next, I play a Bebop-influenced combination of bridging and single approach notes that I used on *G-Spot Blues* from my album *Jazz Metal*. It features a large ascending bridge between A and C# in bars 3-4. Bar five contains a succession of bridging movements that see-saw between C# and E on the same string.

Example 2j

Next, let's shift up to A Mixolydian Shape 4. The series of chromatic bridge movements in this shape could be attributed to a whole host of guitar players from Pat Metheny to George Benson because they fall so comfortably under the hand.

Example 2k

We stay in Shape 4 for another Martino-style example. It uses a series of consecutive chromatic bridges that connect scale notes a tone apart and, again, falls nicely under the fingers.

Example 2l

As you learn more chromatic language, you will start to develop some complex passages by simply joining separate ideas together. The following phrase is just such an example and should be learned as useful short sections that can be isolated and used in other lines and with other shapes.

Example 2m

Example 2n is played in Shape 4, but you might find the fingering too stretchy and complicated. If so, try to relocate various notes until you find a more comfortable position. If everything ends up in Shape 5, learn it as a Shape 5 line.

Example 2n

Example 2o ascends from Shape 4 to Shape 5. Make sure you maintain your visual references throughout, so that you don't get lost, and so you can play it in different keys.

Example 2o

We now shift up to Shape 5.

Example 2p includes a mix of approach notes and bridging moves that fall both on and off the beat, and come from both above and below the target notes. The theme in bars 3-4 is diatonic Country-style 6th intervals linked with chromatic approach notes.

Example 2p

The final line demonstrates some of the ear-bending effects that can be created by a succession of chromatic moves. For a bluesy twist in bar four, we return to the A Minor 6 Pentatonic scale. Watch out for the minor blues curl on the C note.

Example 2q

Chromatic Bridging Solo Study

Bars 1-2

I begin in A Mixolydian Shape 1, before shifting to Shape 2 in bar two, and end up in Shape 5 for bars 3-4. At the end of bar one, an A# is used to bridge B and A which would be easier to see if all three notes were played on the same string. The final two notes of bar four anticipate the C7 in the next bar.

Bars 3-4

No chromatic notes are used here, but notice how the G string bend is held as a pedal tone while the notes above it create a pedal-steel effect.

Bars 5-8

This section features Example 21 transposed to C7. It is reminiscent of Pat Martino's style and is played within C Mixolydian Shape 4.

Bars 9-12

This Johnny Hiland-influenced line features more open string banjo-style ideas. The most difficult aspect is playing the pre-bend in bar twelve without losing momentum.

Bars 13-16

Here, we start in F Mixolydian Shape 4 and end up in Shape 1. Bars 13-14 both feature approach notes from a half step above each target note – a dissonant-sounding option. In bars 15-16, although these bars contain a mixture of above and below chromatic approaches, these simply amount to Mixolydian with an added b3.

Bars 17-20

This Albert Lee-influenced line features a healthy mixture of approach notes and bridging. Bars 17-18 are based on the G Major Blues scale (a Major Pentatonic with an added b3).

G Major Blues Scale	G	A	Bb	B	D	E
Formula	1	2	b3	3	5	6

G Major Blues scale (symmetrical 3-octave pattern)

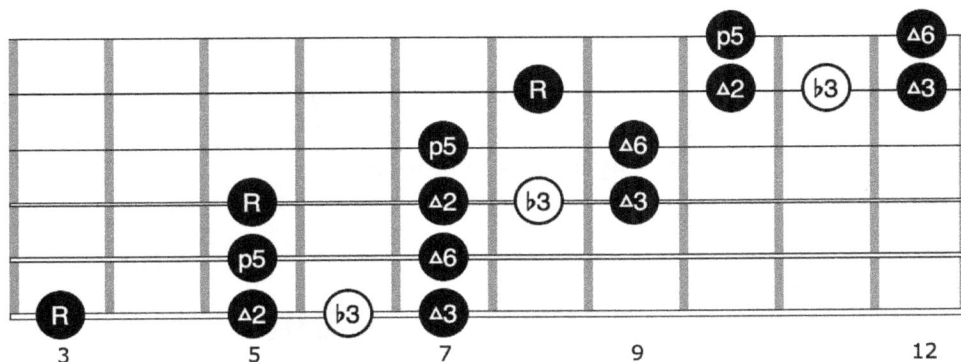

Bars 21-24

This Brent Mason-style line uses lateral movement along the neck, so be aware of which CAGED shape you're in. The final two notes in bar twenty-four are played in anticipation of the C7 in the following bar.

Bars 25-26

There is some respite here from the relentless chromaticism in the form of a sweet C Major Pentatonic-based idea (C, D, E, G, A). This is followed by switching between the darker C Dorian (C, D, Eb, F, G, A, Bb) and a brighter-sounding Mixolydian idea.

C Dorian Shape 5

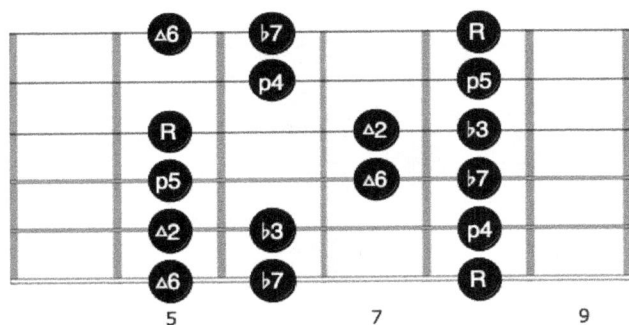

Bars 27-28

Although C Mixolydian with an added b3 is the basis of this Brad Paisley-style lick, I also use a form of bridging. The first note of each triplet is D, Eb and E. In other words, the Eb is used as a bridge between the D and E which act as guide-tones within the line. However, the other Mixolydian notes prolong the movement, a concept called *delayed resolution* that we will explore later.

Bars 29-32

I use another example of delayed resolution in bar thirty-two, where the descending double-stops trace a simple bridging motion between the first and final double-stops.

Bars 33-36

This section features Example 2q transposed to F7 and played in Shape 5. It ends in a bluesy fashion with the use of the F Minor 6 Pentatonic scale for the first four notes of bar thirty-six. Although the A note at the end of bar thirty-six can be seen as the major 3rd of F7, it is actually a pick-up note leading to the G note at the start of the following bar (for G7).

Bars 37-40

I play this passage in open position to give this Brad Paisley-style idea some resonance.

Bars 41-44

In these bars, I play Example 2g shifting from Shape 3 to Shape 2. Again, the A Minor 6 Pentatonic scale is used for a bluesy tinge.

Bars 45-48

The notes within the last two bars of this four-bar section are from the C Major Blues scale.

C Major Blues scale (symmetrical 3-octave pattern)

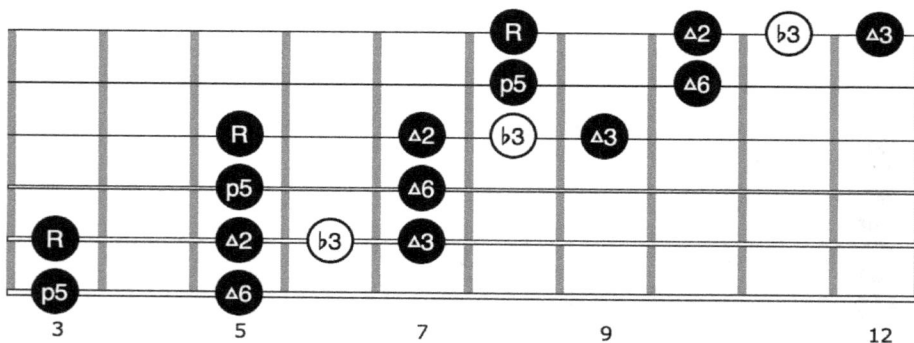

Bars 49-52

The final four notes of bar fifty-two are common to both the D7 and the F7 chord in the following bar.

Bars 53-56

My descending chromatic bridging in bar fifty-four is followed by one that ascends. For more bluesy grime, the F Minor 6 Pentatonic and F Minor Pentatonic scales are used in the second half of bar fifty-five.

Bars 57-60

Think of this section as chromatic bridging within the G Major Pentatonic scale. In this case, I bridge between the 2nd and 3rd (A and B) and the 5th and 6th (D and E).

Bars 61-64

Although most of this section comprises notes of A Mixolydian with various chromatic passing notes, there is a temporary shift to A Minor 6 Pentatonic in bar sixty-two.

Bars 65-68

This section is a modified version of Example 2m transposed to C7. As seen earlier, a descending chromatic bridge is immediately followed by two ascending ones.

Bars 69-72

This section features Example 2j transposed to D7 – a Shape 3 line.

Bars 73-76

This section features Example 2c transposed to F7 and starting on beat 3. There's a lot of chromatic bridging here, starting with an ascent from F to A then back down to Eb. Throughout the line, I always lead into F7 chord tones (F, A, C, Eb)

Bars 77-80

Here, I play Example 2b transposed to G7 concluding in Shape 1 over the G7 chord. Note the temporary transition in bar seventy-nine to the G Minor 6 Pentatonic scale to add some grit with its b3 (Bb).

CHROMATIC BRIDGING SOLO STUDY

[Each chromatic note is indicated with an asterisk]

A.N. = approach-note movement   Br. = bridging

(Shaun Baxter)

G7
Br.
A.N.
Br.
A7
Br.
A.N.
A.N.
BU
A.N.
C7
Let ring
C Dorian
C Mixolydian
C Dorian
D7
P.M.
Br.
Br.
A.N.
A.N.

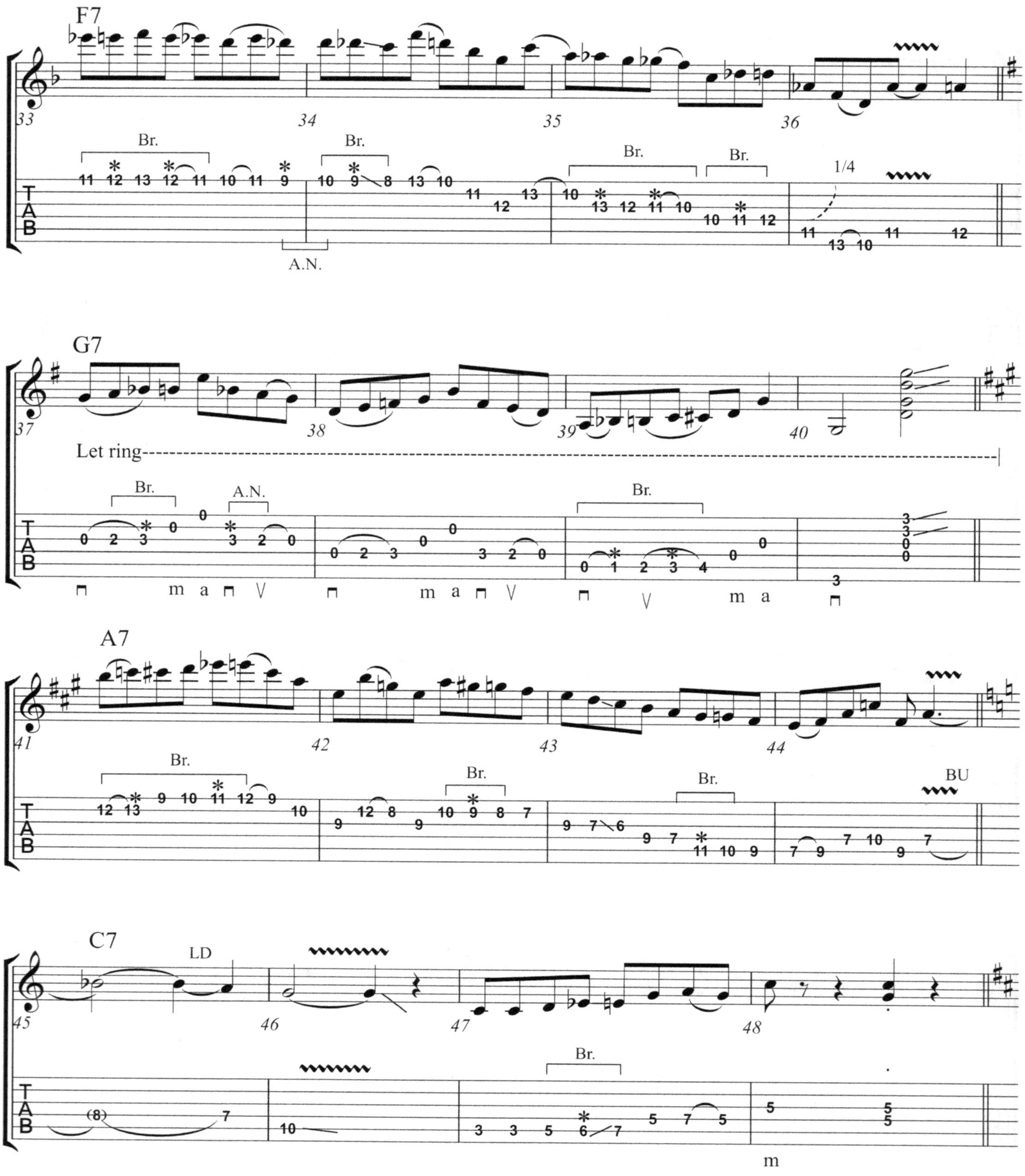
F7
Br.
A.N.
1/4
G7
Let ring
A.N.
A7
BU
C7
LD

D7
A.N.
A.N.
A.N.
Br.
F7
Br.
Br.
1/4 curl
G7
Br.
Br.
Br.
Br.
A7
8va
Loco
A.N
Hold
BU
LD
1/4 curl
Br.
Br.

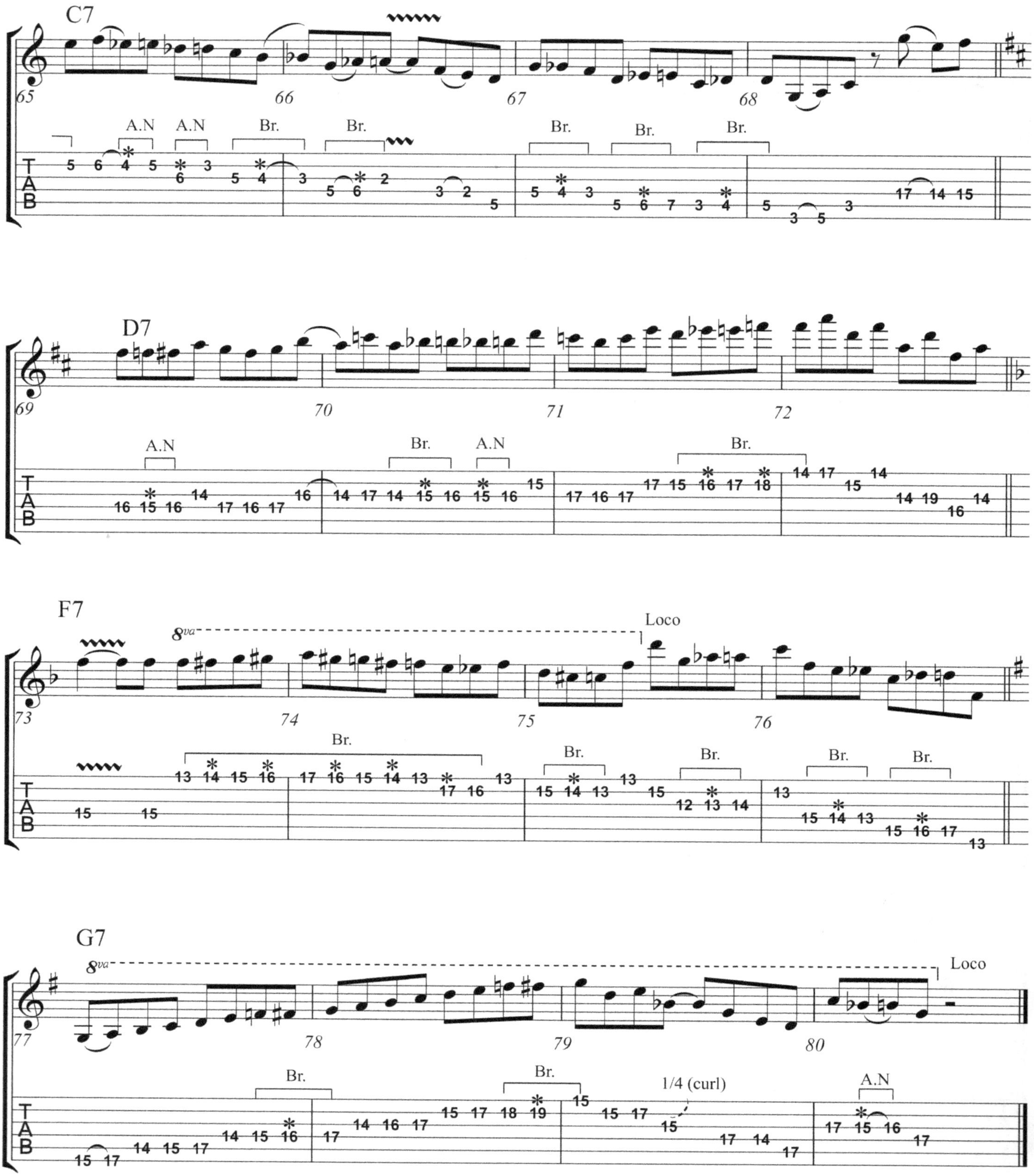
C7
A.N
Br.
D7
F7
8va
Loco
G7
1/4 (curl)
TAB

Chapter Three: Chromatic Enclosure

Now let's explore the idea of a *chromatic enclosure*. This involves approaching a target note from both above *and* below using a combination of notes containing at least one chromatic note.

Diagram 1 shows a selection of two-, three- and four-note combinations that target the note A. The combinations below that feature an asterisk can only be played when the asterisked note is in the scale. Try these on each note while ascending and descending a scale.

2-NOTE APPROACH TO TARGET NOTE

3-NOTE APPROACH TO TARGET NOTE

4-NOTE APPROACH TO TARGET NOTE

* = these notes are only really appropriate when there is a corresponding scale note

A7 CAGED Lines Featuring Chromatic Enclosures

Although enclosures are the main concept here, each example will usually feature some of the other chromatic ideas we've studied so far.

We start with the first of six examples using A Mixolydian Shape 1. It features some three-note enclosures, so see if you can spot which ones are used from the diagram above. The first enclosure in bar one is sometimes referred to as *double chromaticism* because the target note is approached from both a half step above and below.

The second enclosure starts at the end of bar two and is the first of many examples showing how the enclosure units from the diagram above can be arranged over two strings. This can be useful to stop you getting drawn out of position on the neck.

In bar three, I use the repetition of a three-note motif against an 1/8th note rhythm to create an interesting *3 over 4* feel known as a *hemiola*.

Example 3a

In the previous example, the double-chromatic approaches were used to enclose the major 3rd. In this example, I use the same technique to approach the 5th (E) in each octave.

Example 3b

Example 3c begins with a series of four-note enclosures. Notice how the initial note in each enclosure changes depending on whether it is a tone or half step above the target note within A Mixolydian.

Example 3c

Next, I use a mixture of four- and three-note enclosures. Again, I use the 3 over 4 rhythmic effect in the second half of the line.

Example 3d

More three- and four-note enclosures are used in Example 3e. In the first two bars, an 1/8th note rest is played at the end of each four-note motif to create a series of five-note groupings that produce some ear-catching rhythmic displacement and cause the point of emphasis to change throughout.

Example 3e

As each enclosure is five notes long in Example 3f, it allows us to repeat the figure without it sounding overtly repetitive as it creates a natural cross-rhythmic effect.

Example 3f

Now let's start building vocabulary in the other CAGED shapes. This next idea is in Shape 2 and is reminiscent of a classic Bebop figure used by players like Martin Taylor.

Example 3g

The next example demonstrates the virtues of not overdoing things, as it contains a balance of different chromatic approaches mixed with straight arpeggios and scale patterns.

Example 3h

Here's an example of a classic Country line using a combination of chromatic bridging and enclosures to link diatonic 6ths.

Example 3i

Example 3j is the first of three Shape 3 lines. A series of four-note enclosure motifs target each note of an A Major triad.

Example 3j

We target the notes of A Major again in Example 3k, but this time it's via a series of three-note enclosure motifs that create another 3 over 4 feel.

Example 3k

In Example 3l, chromatic notes only ever come from a half step below the target and are always played on the off-beat. In bars 3-4, the groupings are six notes long, which still produces rhythmic displacement, but the effect isn't as radical as the repeating groups of six.

Example 31

This Shape 4 line is based on the same diatonic 6th approach as Example 3i.

Example 3m

The next idea features tight interplay between bridging and enclosure and was inspired by the saxophonist Mornington Lockett.

Example 3n

In this Shape 5 line, a healthy blend of approaches is used to maintain interest.

Example 3o

The accents in this final Shape 5 line provide much of the musicality and interest. It's important to balance all aspects of good line construction when creating your own chromatic-based ideas. This includes things like dynamics, rests, slides, bends and vibrato. Also consider how much you balance diatonic and chromatic ideas, as heavily chromatic music can be somewhat exhausting for your audience to listen to.

Example 3p

Chromatic Enclosures Solo Study

Before working your way through this analysis, it is worth noting that any enclosure can often be seen as a combination of approach notes and bridging patterns, so I've analysed the transcription using my own perspective on what I'm playing. Don't worry if you see it differently!

Bars 1-4

This first section is a modified version of Example 3b. Both enclosures feature a chord tone approached by two chromatic notes (one a half step above and one a half step below). This same motion can be seen again throughout the piece.

Bars 5-8

Bar five features the same enclosure motif as bars two and three and is followed by several descending and ascending chromatic bridges. In bar eight, you'll see that two chromatic approaches overlap.

Bars 9-12

These bars are a modified version of Example 3c transposed to D7 and relocated to Shape 4.

I play a series of four-note enclosures, each formed from a scale note immediately above the target note, then the target note itself, then a chromatic note a half step below the target note, then the target note again.

In bar twelve, the enclosure motif combines elements of the two we've seen so far. As with the ones in bars two, three and five, it contains three notes, but like the ones in bars 9-10 it begins with a scale note immediately above the target note.

Bars 13-16

This section features Example 3l transposed to F7.

In bars 13-14, I play a four-note enclosure that comprises a scale note a half step above the target note, a scale note a whole step below the target, a chromatic note a half step below the target, then finally the target note itself.

The three-note enclosures in bars 15-16 form part of larger six-note groupings that create cross rhythmic interest.

Bars 17-20

The enclosure motif in bars seventeen and nineteen is similar to the one in bars two, three and five, but this time played within double-stops. Focus on what's happening on the G string.

Bars 21-24

From the second half of bar twenty-three, I play a Shape 3 A Minor 6 Pentatonic scale line followed by an A Minor Pentatonic idea.

Bars 25-28

The enclosure in bar twenty-seven is an example of *double chromaticism* where the note C is approached via a chromatic note both a half step above and below.

Bars 29-32

The first and second enclosure figures in this section are the same, but played an octave apart. The third of D7 (F#) is targeted, first from a scale note a half step above (G), then from a scale note below (E), and finally a chromatic note from below (F).

Bars 33-36

Here, I play Example 2d transposed to F7. The final note in this section anticipates the G7 in the following bar.

Bars 37-40

The first enclosure motif is three notes long and starts with a chromatic note a half step below the target note, then a scale note a whole step above the target note, then the target note.

Bars 41-44

In this section, I play Example 2a – a simple descent of the A Bebop scale followed by an ascending A7 arpeggio idea. The final note in this bar (C) is played in anticipation of the C7 in the following bar.

Bars 45-48

This section is built around Example 3e transposed to C7. Notice how I create rhythmic interest by holding the final note of each bridging motif twice as long as the preceding ones to create a five-note grouping.

Bars 49-52

From bar fifty, I play a modified version of Example 2n transposed to D7. The final note (F) anticipates the F7 in the following bar.

Bars 53-56

Here I play a modified version of Example 2h, not only transposed from A7 to F7, but also relocated from Shape 3 to Shape 5.

Bars 57-60

In beat 3 of bar fifty-seven, I begin a modified version of Example 3h that's transposed to G7.

Towards the end of bar fifty-seven, I use a four-note enclosure motif that comprises, a scale note a whole step above the target, then a chromatic note a half step above the target note, then a scale note a half step below the target note before finally landing on the target.

Bars 61-64

This section is a rhythmically-displaced version of Example 3i.

Bars 65-68

As a respite from the relentless chromaticism, this section contains just one approach note. In bar sixty-seven, the first six notes imply a G7#5 chord (the V of C7), which adds some harmonic interest and propulsion to by imposing a perfect cadence with the melody.

Bars 69-72

The double-stops here create a minor to major tension and relief effect as I alternate between two-note fragments of D Minor and D Major. Rhythmic interest is created by mixing groups of five and six played as even 1/8th notes.

Bars 73-76

The final section uses Example 3a transposed to F7.

I use a series of consecutive three-note enclosures, each comprising a scale note a whole step above the target, then a chromatic note a half step below the target, then the target note.

Bars 77-80

The solo concludes in resonant fashion with the inclusion of several open-string ideas.

CHROMATIC ENCLOSURES SOLO STUDY

[Each chromatic note is indicated with an asterisk]

A.N. = approach-note movement   Br. = bridging   Enc. = enclosure

(Shaun Baxter)

G7
Br.
Enc.
Br.
Enc.
A7
Br.
Enc.
1/4 (curl)
1/4 (curl)
C7
A.N.
Br.
Br.
Br.
Enc.
D7
A.N.
A.N.
A.N.
A.N.
Br.
Br.
Enc.
Enc.

F7
Br.
A.N.
G7
Br.
A.N.
Ring---|
Ring-|
Enc.
Enc.
Enc.
A.N.
A.N.
Br.
A7
Br.
Br.
A.N.
Hold --|
Enc.
C7
(5)
(5)
(5)
Br.
A.N.
Br.
Br.
Br.
Br.
A.N.
Enc.

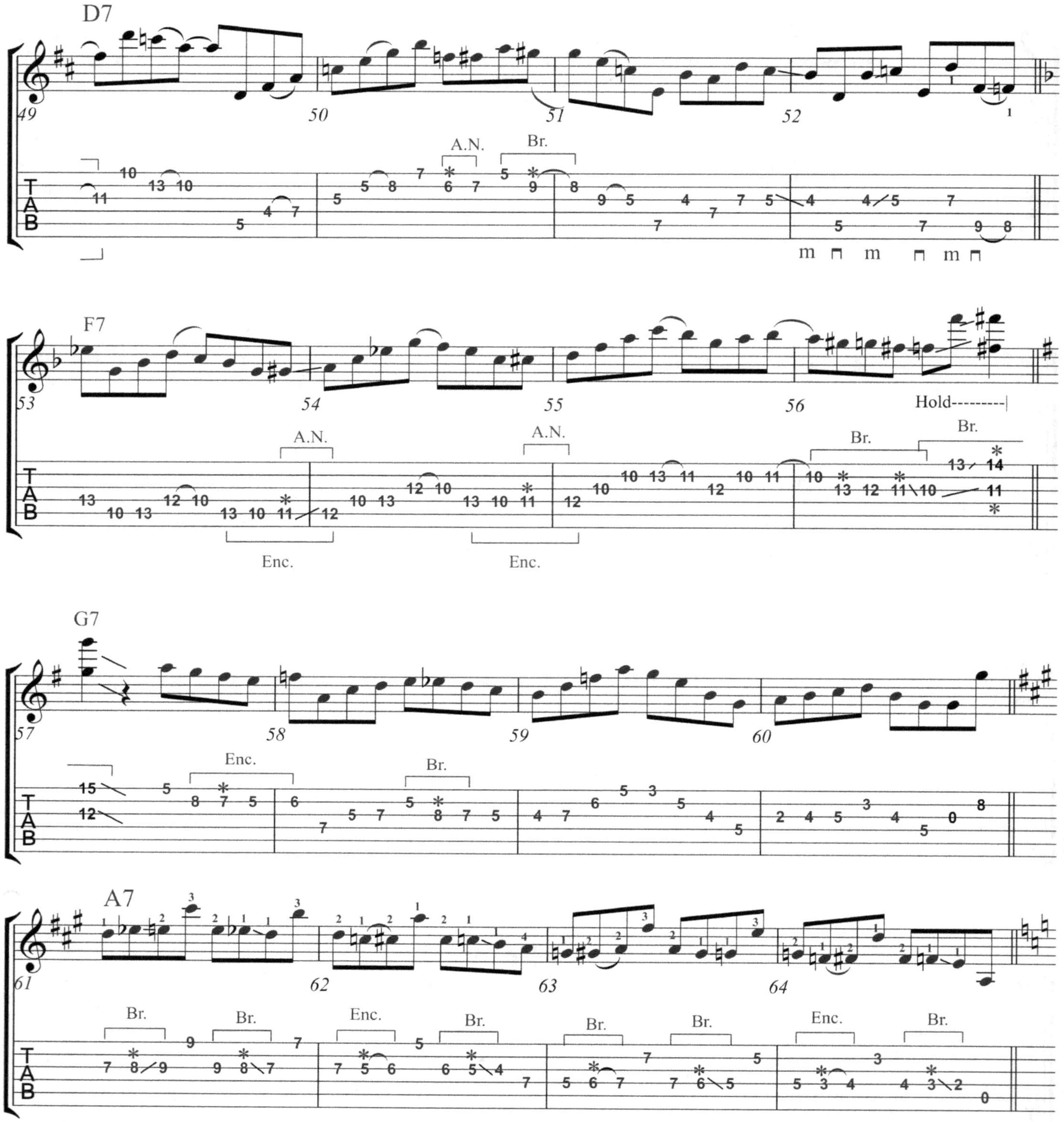
D7
A.N.
Br.
F7
A.N.
Br.
Enc.
Hold
G7
Enc.
Br.
A7
Br.
Enc.
TAB

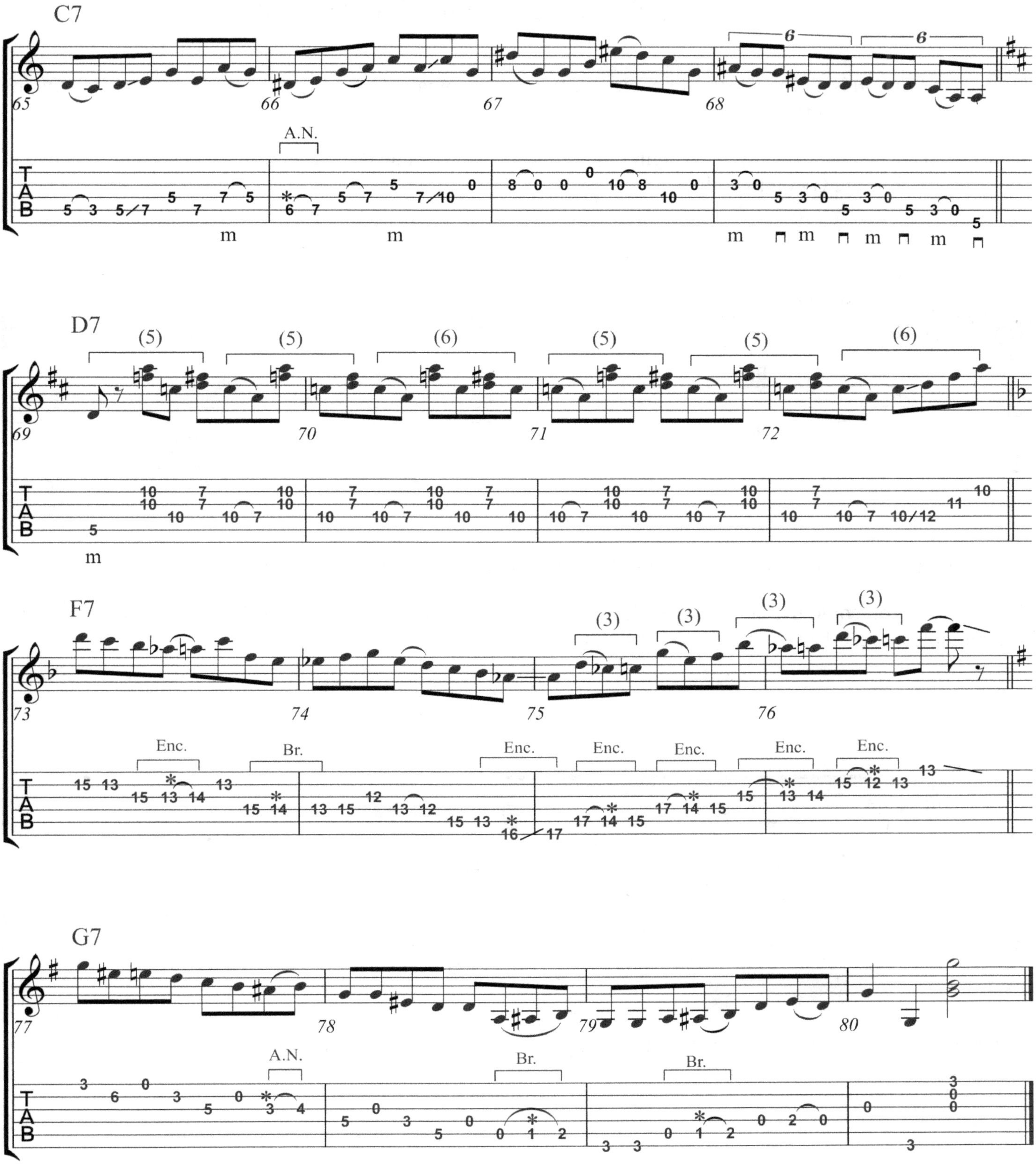
C7
A.N.
D7
F7
Enc.
Br.
G7

Chapter Four: Delayed Resolution

Delayed resolution is a specific type of enclosure where a chromatic journey is extended or interrupted by one or more notes from another string.

For example, imagine a chromatic bridging move from the note A on the 7th fret of the D string to resolve to G on the 5th fret, via G# on the 6th fret.

This motion can be extended using surrounding scale notes to delay the resolution.

For example, you could use an E on the 7th fret of the A string as a lower pedal tone between each of the three original notes to get the sequence A, E, G#, E, G.

You could also play the same idea with the E played an octave higher on the 9th fret of the G string.

A7

In fact, you can safely add almost any other scale note to a chromatic sequence to lengthen, disguise, and ultimately delay its resolution to the target. In this chapter we will explore various ways to do that and see how to create your own musical ideas.

A7 CAGED Lines Featuring Delayed Resolution

Once again, we will study delayed resolution lines in each of the five CAGED shapes of A Mixolydian.

We begin in Shape 1 with a line reminiscent of Jazz master Joe Pass. Here, my straightforward chromatic ascent G, G#, A is interrupted by a brief diversion to B on the 3rd string. I then play the same idea on D, D#, and E by adding the F# on the fourth string.

Example 4a

In the following Pat Martino-influenced example, we transition down from Shape 1 to Shape 3. The delayed resolution passage shows how my descending chromatic motion of F#, F, E on the A string is interrupted by C#.

Example 4b

Next, the ascending chromatic motion of C#, D, D#, E on the A string is delayed by a brief diversion to an F# on the D string. This is followed in similar fashion a 4th higher when the ascending chromatic motion of F#, G, G#, A on the D string is briefly delayed by the B on the G string.

Example 4c

So far, all the chromatic motion has been embellished using one note from a string above or below. Now we're going to look at two variations on that theme using ideas in Shape 2.

The delayed resolution in bar two shows how the descending motion of C#, C, B is delayed via two notes on the B string. The idea in bar three adds a scale note on strings both above and below the descending chromatic motion on the G string.

Example 4d

This Shape 2 idea begins in Shape 1 and features *contrary motion* on two different strings.

In the first bar, I play a descending G, F#, F, E line on the B string combined with an ascending line of C, C#, D, D# on the G string (which resolves to E on the B string).

In bar two, the ascending motion of E, F, F#, G on the B string runs in parallel with the descending chromatic series of Eb, D, Db, C#, C, B on the G string.

The line finishes off with approach notes to each note of an A Major triad.

Example 4e

This Shape 2 line is reminiscent of Pat Martino and here the descending motion of F#, F, G on the B string is embellished with a D on the G string.

Example 4f

Next, I use a D on the G string as a pedal tone to embellish the G, F#, F, E chromatic descent on the B string.

Example 4g

Our final Shape 2 line is Charlie Parker-influenced and similar to the previous one. Here, a B on the D string is used as a pedal tone to embellish the E, Eb, D, C# descent on the G string.

Example 4h

The following Shape 3 Pat Martino-style example also uses a pedal point. In the first two bars, a D repeatedly interrupts the chromatic descent of F#, F, E on the G string.

Example 4i

In Example 4j, the chromatic descent on the B string is diverted briefly by the G note on the G string.

Example 4j

On to Shape 4. My descending chromatic motion on the high E string of G, F#, F, E is briefly delayed by a D on the B string. In bar four, a C# on the D string offers a brief interruption to the F#, F, E chromatic descent on the G string.

Example 4k

In Example 4l, I play an ascending chromatic series of notes on the D string embellished by three other notes on the string above.

Example 4l

Example 4m is situated somewhere between shapes 4 and 5 of A Mixolydian and is influenced by Jazz pianist Elaine Elias. Here, an E on the D string is used as a pedal point to my chromatic descent on the G string. The bluesy finish in bar five uses the A Minor 6 Pentatonic scale.

Example 4m

In the first two bars of Example 4n, our first Shape 5 idea, my three-note chromatic descent of F#, F and E on the E string is embellished with a C# on the B string.

Example 4n

Finally, the D on the A string is used as a pedal point embellishment to a chromatic descent of G, F#, F, E on the D string.

Example 4o

Delayed Resolution Solo Study

While this solo contains many examples of delayed resolution, it also features each of the chromatic devices we've studied so far, namely approach notes, bridging and enclosures.

With each four-bar section, contextualise *everything* that you play. What CAGED shape(s) are you using? What key are you in? Which chromatic ideas are played? If you lose awareness of these elements, you will not be able to apply what you learn to other keys. It might feel as though this process slows you down at first, but soon you will speed up and reap the benefits.

Bars 1-4

This section is formed from a modified version of Example 4i. My first three notes on the G string form a chromatic descent of F#, F, E, which is interrupted by a repeated D pedal note on the 12th fret.

Bars 5-8

The first two bars are a modified version of Example 4b transposed to C7. The four-note enclosure in bar seven targets G using two scale notes from above (Bb and A) and a chromatic note from a half step below (F#). The final D in bar eight is a pick-up note relating to the D7 in bar nine.

Bars 9-12

Bar ten contains two chromatic lines (a descent from the 7th, 6th and 5th frets on the G and E strings) that are effectively interrupted by each other.

Bars 13-16

Bar fourteen begins a chromatic descent from D to C via a C# passing note. This movement is delayed by the C on the D string. In bar sixteen, a descent from E to D via a chromatic C# is delayed via the insertion of the Bb and A notes on the D string.

Bars 17-20

In bar eighteen, I play two chromatic descents, each interrupting and delaying the other.

You could view this line as a diatonic third (E to G) moving down to another diatonic third (D to F) via a chromatic third (Eb to F#). In bar nineteen, I switch to a darker-sounding G Dorian for a bit of contrast.

At the end of bar twenty, the journey on the D string from G to A via G# is interrupted and delayed by a repeated pedal note on a higher string.

Bars 21-24

I build this section around Example 4a and it begins with a transposed version of the same four-note delayed resolution motif. Both motifs here can also be seen as enclosures.

Bars 25-28

These bars feature Example 4m played in C7 only with a modified start and ending.

Bars 29-32

Hopefully, you are starting to know what to look for by now. In bar thirty-one, a chromatic descent from E to D via Eb is delayed by the addition of a C on the D string.

Bars 33-36

This section contains another use of Example 4l, this time transposed to F7. In bar thirty-three, I play a chromatic ascent from a Bb to a C natural at the start of bar thirty-four. This motion is delayed by inserting various notes on the adjacent G string.

Bars 37-40

Here, I use Example 4g transposed to G7 with a modified beginning.

Bars 41-44

My double-stops in bar forty-two comprise a chromatic descent that is delayed by a note added below. In bar forty-four, I play a chromatic ascent of B, C, C# on the A string which is extended with the inclusion of several open A strings.

Bars 49-52

This is Example 4c transposed to D7.

Bars 53-56

This section features Example 4d played in F7. At the start of bar fifty-four, a chromatic descent from A to G is extended and delayed by a D and F on the adjacent B string.

Bars 57-60

Here I play Example 4h transposed to G7.

Bars 61-64

In this section, each eight-note grouping contains a four-note delayed resolution motif with the second played an octave lower than the first. Focus on the first and last note of each motif and you'll see how the chromatic motion is delayed by notes on adjacent lower strings.

Bars 65-68

These four bars feature Example 4o transposed to C7.

Bars 69-72

A straightforward enclosure movement can be disguised when the notes are played on a different string. Across bars seventy and seventy-one, I approach the A from a half step below and a whole step above.

Bars 73-76

Note how the last three notes of bar seventy-six also relate to the G7 in the following bar.

Bars 77-80

Finally, for a bit of fun to end the solo, I play Example 4e transposed to G7. This idea contains contrary motion where one chromatic line moves down, then up the B string, while a second moves up and down the G string. Effectively, both lines are interrupted and delayed by each other.

DELAYED RESOLUTION SOLO STUDY

[Each chromatic note is indicated with an asterisk]

(Shaun Baxter)

'Del. Res' = delayed resolution   'Enc.' = enclosure   'Br.' = bridging   'A.N.' = approach-note

G7
(G)
A.N.
(G7#5)
Del. Res.
(C)
(G)
Del. Res. (Enc.)
A7
Del. Res. (Enc.)
Enc.
C7
Br.
Del. Res.
D7
A.N.
Enc.
Del. Res.

F7
Del. Res.
Enc.
Br.
Br.
Del. Res.
G7
Br.
Br.
Del. Res.
Br.
A.N.
A7
A.N.
Hold-----|
Del. Res.
Del. Res.
C7
(3)
(3)
(3)
Hold--|
Hold-----|
Hold--------|
A.N.
A.N.
Del. Res.
A.N.
A.N.
A.N.
A.N.

D7
(7)
(7)
Del. Res.
A.N.
Del. Res.
A.N.
Br.
Br.
Br.
F7
A.N.
A.N.
Del. Res.
Del. Res.
G7
Br.
Del. Res.
Hold--|
A.N.
Hold--|
A.N.
A7
(8)
(8)
A.N.
A.N.
Del. Res.
A.N.
Del. Res.
A.N.
Hold----|

C7
Hold--|
Del. Res.
Enc.
Hold--|
D7
Bridging
Enc.
Del. Res.
F7
BU
G7
Del. Res.
Del. Res.
A.N.
A.N.
A.N.
A.N.

Chapter Five: Twelve-Tone Rows

12-tone music (also known as *dodecaphony*) is a compositional device invented by Austrian classical composer Josef Matthias Hauer in the early part of the 20th century. The intention was to break away from the traditional hierarchy of key-orientated harmony, where some notes in a scale are stronger than others, in order to give equal importance to each of the twelve chromatic notes.

This technique was used extensively by Arnold Schoenberg and his students (such as Alban Berg and Anton Webern) and even into the 1950s and '60s by composers like Pierre Boulez and Igor Stravinsky.

The atonal effects of the 12-tone method of composing are also ideal for dark styles like black- and death-metal, and with the increasingly complex genre of "Math Rock".

The technique involves arranging the twelve notes of the chromatic scale in any order of your choice. This series becomes a set *tone row*. The rule is that, once a note has been played it cannot be played again until all the remaining eleven have been used (although you can repeat it as many times as you like before moving on to the subsequent notes).

In classical music, once the *tone row* has been established, it serves as the basis of the music's melodies, counterpoint and harmony.

The way that this technique differs from the other chromatic concepts is that:

• The period of dissonance is extended (for a full twelve notes before resolution)

• For the duration of the note row, there is no tonal hierarchy (i.e., there is no functional distinction between scale notes and non-scale notes)

As well as using the tone row in its original form, it may also undergo certain *transformations*. You can play it:

• **Backwards** (*retrograde*)

• **Upside down** (*inversion*), so that a rising minor third becomes a falling minor third, etc.

• **Both backwards and upside down** (*retrograde inversion*)

As guitarists, we can apply this technique in a more diatonic setting by resolving each line back home to the parental scale.

Because they are atonal (keyless), a tone row idea can be transposed to begin on any note of the chromatic scale. However, keep in mind that some lines will sound more consonant than others, depending on the melodic and rhythmic placement of the notes that are inside or outside of the key.

For example, if you construct a 12-tone row where each chromatic note is used as a means of passing to a scale note, it will sound quite consonant in that key.

For this chapter, it will best serve the concept of tone rows to jump straight into a solo and see it in action, so we'll move directly to the solo study section.

Twelve-Tone Row Solo Study

This solo study could well be the first time that tone rows have been applied to Country Rock music! Imagine what Freddie Kruger might play if he were a hillbilly guitar player. The challenge being: if we can make it work in this setting, it can work anywhere!

In my solo, you'll see each 12-tone row flanked and resolved with the Mixolydian scale over each chord. This ties the extreme chromaticism back to the key and helps to resolve each dissonant phrase to the chord.

Once you have learned the solo, experiment with your own tone-row sequences and try the various transformation methods (inversion, retrograde and retrograde inversion) to generate more material from each idea.

Bars 0-4

I begin by descending through all 12 chromatic notes in order, but notice how I start and finish on chord-tones relating to the underlying A7. The final nine notes of this section are taken from A Minor Pentatonic scale.

Bars 5-8

It may not look or sound like it, but here I play a straight ascent of the Chromatic Scale starting from C, which is disguised by switching octaves on different notes – an ear-catching technique known as *octave dispersal*. Pat Martino calls this approach *octavism* and also refers to it as *spatial fingerings*.

Bars 9-10

In this section, the gravitational pull moves from the *inside* (D Mixolydian) to the *outside* (C# Major Pentatonic scale) before resolving back to D Mixolydian. If you add all the notes of C# Major Pentatonic to D Mixolydian you get all twelve tones.

Bars 11-12

Here, I play two divergent chromatic lines: one descending and the other ascending.

Although the first 12 notes are the tone row, the sequence has been continued for another four notes at the end of bar twelve. I use hybrid picking, but it's not essential, so use alternate- or economy-picking if you prefer.

Everything resolves in bar twelve, and the final two notes are chord-tones of D7, which I slide up a minor third to target the following F7.

Bars 13-16

In bars 14-16, I play two twelve-tone rows back to back. Notice the repetition of the same four-note motif played a half step lower in the second note row.

Bars 17-20

This passage starts with an ascending chromatic sequence – the opposite approach to the one I used in bars 1-2.

Bars 21-22

Not only do I use octave dispersal in this section, I also play about with the note order in each four-note cell too and move up in major 3rds.

Bars 23-24

From the third beat of bar twenty-three, I play a symmetrical passage in which a 12-tone row is created by moving the same four-note motif down in whole steps.

Bars 25-28

The 12-tone row in the first two bars of this section can be seen as fitting around Mixolydian Shape 3.

Bars 29-32

As with bars 23-24, the note-row that begins in bar thirty comprises a four-note motif that's taken through the scale in whole tones. However, this time I ascend instead of descending.

Bars 33-36

The two note rows in these bars are completely random! I've basically taken all twelve notes and used my ears to come up with something interesting and (hopefully) expressive.

Bars 37-40

In bars 38-39, there's a good example of convergent motion (moving together) as the notes of the chromatic descending and ascending lines eventually meet up.

Bars 41-44

I return to the same principle used in bars 9-10, only this time with A Mixolydian and the five remaining notes of the twelve-tone row that form G# Major Pentatonic (G#, A#, B#, D#, E#). These are used to take the line somewhat "outside" the tonality.

Bars 45-48

In the latter two bars, the 12-tone row is inserted within other notes from C Mixolydian around Shape 2.

Bars 49-52

This is a re-application of the principle used in bar thirty, but with this particular pattern, I have had to replace the anticipated F# (14th fret) at the end with a C because F# was already played at the start of the row.

Bars 53-56

Here's another example of divergent chromatic motion, but this time the ascending line is ahead of the descending one. Again, like bars 5-6, 11-12 and 21-23, the logic of the note row is extended beyond the confines of the initial twelve notes.

Bars 57-60

It's possible to divide a 12-note row into four triad structures, rather than see it as a set of random single notes. These provide more harmonic strength to each 12-tone series because you can start thinking about chords instead of 12-note melodies. In bars 57-59, both note-rows use the triads Gm, Am, B and C#.

Bars 61-64

The note row in the first two bars starts with some convergent chromatic motion (descending on the B string and ascending on the G string). The dissonance of the 12-tone row is resolved by using pure A Mixolydian in bars 63-64.

Bars 65-68

In bars 67-68, I use a descending version of the ascending octave dispersion approach from bars 5-6.

Bars 69-72

Here, view the 12-tone row in relation to D Mixolydian Shape 2. This will help you to see where dissonance occurs, resolve the line accordingly, and apply it to other keys by thinking of it as a Shape 2 chromatic line.

Bars 73-76

There are more fun and games in the first two bars of this section as I ascend chromatically on the B string while descending chromatically on G string. Although the whole thing can be seen as a giant delayed resolution figure, it does contain 12 different notes, so it's a *bona fide* 12-tone row. This one lives around Mixolydian Shape 1 and resolves to chord tones of F Major.

Bars 77-80

Finally, I round things off by returning to the divergent chromatic motion used earlier in bars 53-54. This time, the fingering is different and we exit via some wide double-stops.

12-TONE ROW SOLO STUDY

[Each chromatic note is indicated with an asterisk]

A.N. = approach-note movement   Br. = bridging   Enc. = enclosure

(Shaun Baxter)

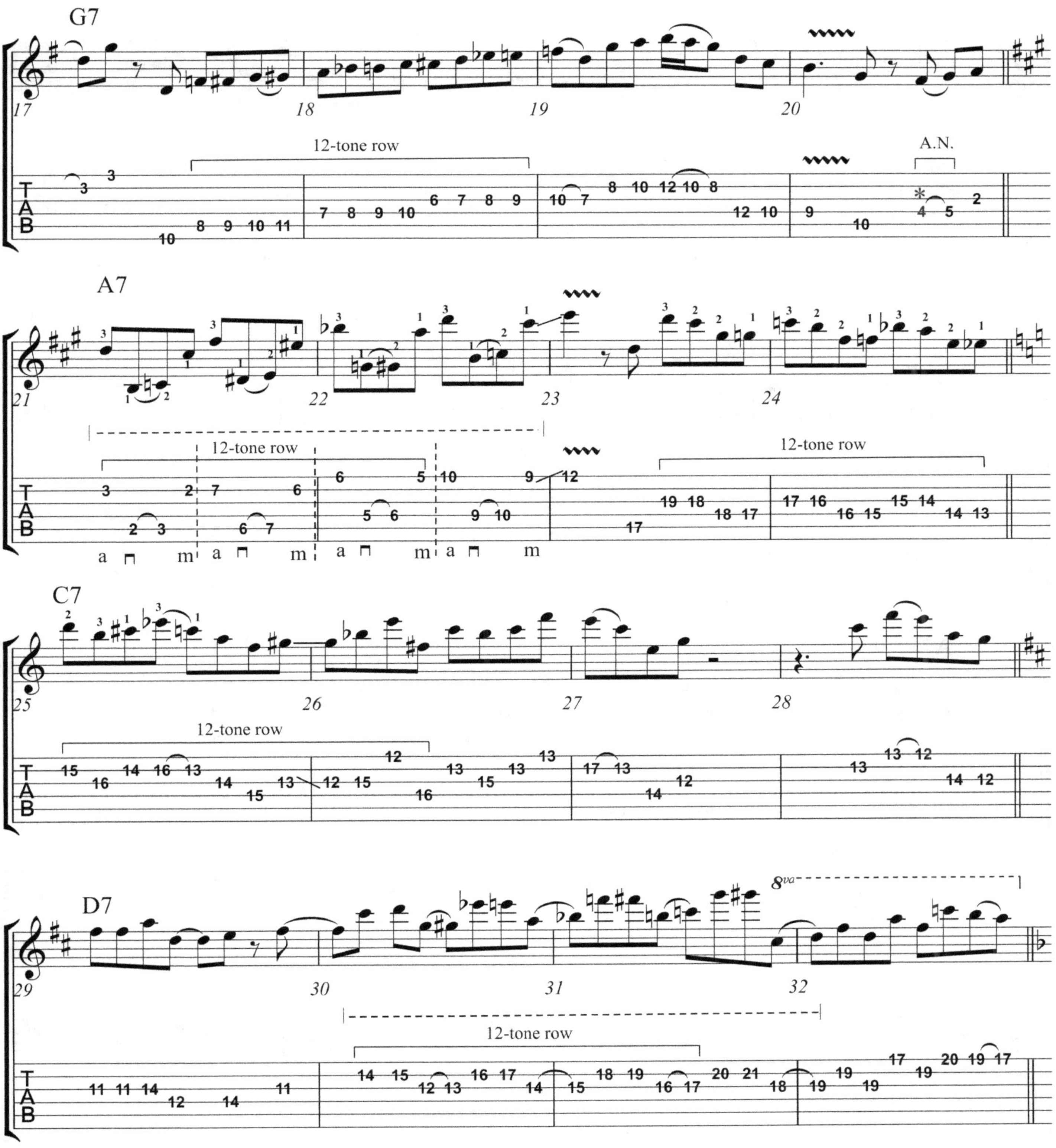
G7
12-tone row
A.N.
A7
12-tone row
C7
12-tone row
D7
8va
12-tone row

F7
BU
12-tone row
Enclosure
12-tone row
G7
Convergent chromatic motion
12-tone row
1/4 (curl)
G minor blues scale
A7
12-tone row
A mixolydian
G# major pent.
Br.
C7
12-tone row

D7
Br.
12-tone row
8va
F7
Divergent chromatic motion
12-tone row
BU
LD
Hold
BU
PB20
G7
12-tone row
12-tone row
Gm
Am
B
C#
Gm
Am
B
C#
A7
12-tone row

C7
(5)
(5)
(5)
Octave dispersal
Br.
12-tone row
D7
12-tone row
Del. Res.
8va
F7
12-tone row
Del. Res.
Br.
G7
Divergent chromatic motion
Hold
12-tone row

Chapter Six: Mixed Chromatic Techniques

We've covered five different ways to spice up lines using chromatic notes and, in this final chapter, you will apply all of them to a couple of solo studies. To recap, we've covered:

- **Chromatic Approach Notes:** either from a half step above or below the target note

- **Chromatic Bridging:** where one scale is linked to another by a consecutive series of chromatic steps

- **Chromatic Enclosures:** approaching a target note from both above *and* below using one or more chromatic notes, often in conjunction with diatonic notes

- **Delayed Resolution:** incorporating notes from one or more other strings (that often act as pedal tones) to delay the chromatic journey to a target note

- **12-tone rows:** the practice of arranging the 12 notes of the Chromatic Scale in any order of your choice to form a set *tone row*. Once a note has been played, it cannot be returned to until all remaining eleven notes have been used

Mixed Chromatic Techniques Solo Study One

Bars 1-4

Although this solo study is designed to demonstrate chromaticism, I feel it is important to write something musical that offers variety and balance, so in the opening four bars I set the mood by using pure Mixolydian before the chromatic mayhem ensues. Various open strings are used "banjo style", so make sure you fret each note with your fingertips to let each one ring.

Bars 5-8

The bulk of this Brent Mason-influenced line is taken from C Mixolydian Shape 5.

Although bar seven could be explained in terms of an enclosure, it's probably more appropriate to see it as implying a *perfect cadence* (G7 to C7) in the melody to add some harmonic direction.

In bar eight, my chromatic ascent from a C Major triad to a D Major triad (in bar nine) via a C# Major, is broken up by splitting each triad into double-stops and using each 5th interval as a bass note.

Bars 9-12

We're back to the harmonic respite of pure Mixolydian in this Brent Mason-style double-stop riff. Notice the rhythmic interest added by the 6:6:4 groupings in each bar.

Bars 13-16

In bar fourteen, my chromatic descent of double-stops is delayed by the addition of an F on the D string. I switch from F Mixolydian to the darker sounding F Dorian from the second half of bar fifteen.

Bars 17-20

Most of the first half of this passage is formed from the notes of G Major Pentatonic (G Mixolydian with no 4th or b7th).

Bars 21-24

You may want to play the double-stops in bars 21-22 using hybrid picking.

Remember to view each line as built around a particular shape. The second half of this passage lives in A Mixolydian Shape 5.

Bars 23-24 demonstrates another example of how an enclosure can be seen as a combination of bridging and approach notes.

Bars 25-28

Along with the chromatic bridging moves, I add more darkness to the end of this line with the C Minor 6 Pentatonic scale.

Bars 29-32

It's not just the banjo and pedal steel that are mimicked by Country guitar players. This line was influenced by some Country fiddle double-stops.

Bars 33-36

This section features Example 4n transposed to F7.

Bars 37-40

Stacked minor 3rds on the top four strings form the theme of these four bars. I build these from the G Half-Whole scale as it contains many useful chromatic tensions.

G Half-Whole	G	Ab	A#	B	C#	D	E	F
Formula	1	b2	#2	3	#4	5	6	b7

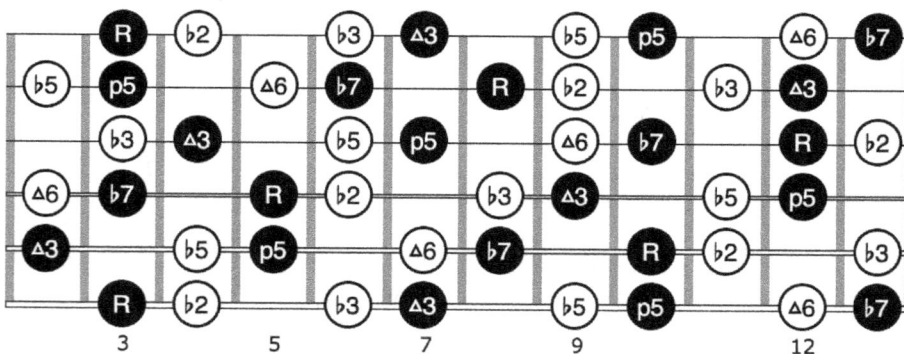

When using the Half Whole scale in this context, you can view the #4 interval as a bluesy b5 and the #2 as an equally bluesy b3. It's only the b2 that has any real dissonance. Once the three-note motif is introduced at the start of bar thirty-nine, the listener will readily accept the symmetrical thematic development that follows.

Bars 41-48

In this passage, I show how Mixolydian can be brought to life with a pedal steel-style approach. This line requires great accuracy with the intonation of the various bends as each one played at speed.

Bars 49-52

This Martino-style line is another example of octave dispersal and involves a straight descent of the Chromatic Scale with the notes shifted into different octaves. As Martino likes to end a tone-row back on the first note it actually creates a 13-note line, so rhythmic displacement occurs as each 13-note motif shifts by one 1/8th note when it is repeated.

Bars 53-56

I take a melodic breather in F Mixolydian here with just a gentle chromatic bridge between two chord tones towards the end of bar fifty-six.

Bars 57-60

At this point I am playing 12-tone rows so there is no hierarchical distinction here between scale notes and chromatic notes.

Bars 61-64

The bend in bar 64 should be pulled down so that the E can ring out to create a pedal steel effect. The same approach is used in bars sixty-nine and eighty.

Bars 65-68

The five-note groupings in bar sixty-six let me repeat the same idea without sounding repetitive. Again, rhythmic displacement creates a constant shift in emphasis that helps to disguise that I'm repeating the same idea.

Bars 69-72

This section is not as chromatically dense as other passages but it does offer a good balance of D Mixolydian, chromatic bridging and D Minor Pentatonic.

Bars 73-76

Notice how the 12-tone row features the descent of a dominant pentatonic scale idea: Eb Dominant Pentatonic descends to D Dominant Pentatonic, then to Db Dominant Pentatonic, before alighting on something close to C Dominant Pentatonic which lives within F Mixolydian.

Bars 77-80

I conclude with more banjo-style open strings in bars 77-78 and some pedal steel-style double-stop bends in bars 79-80.

MIXED CHROMATIC TECHNIQUES SOLO STUDY #1

[Each chromatic note is indicated with an asterisk]

G7
Br.
BU
PB10
LD
A.N.
A7
Hold---------|
A.N.
BU
Br.
A.N.
Br.
Enc
C7
Br.
Br.
Br.
Cm6 pentatonic
D7
Ring---|
Ring---|
Ring---|
Ring--------------|
Ring---|
Ring---|
Ring---|
Ring--------|
BU
LD
A.N.

F7
Del. Res.
Br.
Br.
Br.
Enc.
G7
G Half-whole scale
A7
Ring
BU
BU
BU
BU
BU
BU
BU
PB16
BU
C7
Enc.
A.N.
A.N.

D7
(13)
(13)
12-tone row - octave dispersal
12-tone row - octave dispersal
A.N.
F7
BU
Br.
G7
12-tone row
12-tone row
A7
A.N.
Br.
A.N.
Hold
Enc.
BD

C7
(5)
(5)
(5)
(5)
(4)
Enc.
Enc.
Enc.
Enc.
Enc.
D7
Hold
BD
LB
Br.
Dm pent.
Br.
F7
(5)
(5)
12-tone row
G7
A.N.
A.N.
m
m
A.N.
BU
PB14
PB14
PB15
Br
LD
Hold
BU (slowly)

Mixed Chromatic Techniques Solo Study Two

Bars 1-4

The first two bars are based around A Mixolydian Shape 1. The consecutive bridging motifs in bars 3-4 are made more ear-catching and "countryfied" by using open strings to add a pedal-steel effect. You'll see this idea throughout the piece.

Bars 5-8

Here, the first two bars are based around Shape 5 of C7 and although it can be viewed as C Mixolydian with chromatic approach notes, I was really thinking of the C Major Blues scale (C Major Pentatonic with an added b3). The melody in bars 7-8 outlines a G7alt chord, the dominant chord of C.

Bars 9-12

Bars 9-10 are based around D Minor Pentatonic and 11-12 are based around D Mixolydian Shape 4.

Bars 13-16

Here's another example of how a chromatic move can be viewed from two different perspectives. In this case, it could be a three-note bridge or a four-note enclosure. The passing notes in bars 15-16 are b3 and b5: a common interplay between F Mixolydian and F Minor Blues.

Bars 17-20

Again, the open strings add interest to this section, including the chromatic approach note in bar seventeen. In bars 19-20, I reintroduce the G Half-Whole scale and the final four notes in bar twenty are played in anticipation of the A7 chord in the following bar.

Bars 21-24

This 12-tone row is formed of identical four-note motifs repeated in leaps of a major third lower. The final three notes in bar twenty-four are played in anticipation of the D7 in the following bar.

Bars 25-28

Both enclosures in bars 25-26 could be seen as a C Lydian Dominant scale if you find that more convenient.

C Lydian Dominant	C	D	E	F#	G	A	Bb
Formula	1	2	3	#4	5	6	b7

Bars 29-32

This 12-tone row is based on a chromatic descent disguised by octave dispersal. For a darker sound, my final four notes in bar thirty-two are taken from the D Minor Blues scale.

Bars 33-36

Here, I play Example 1h transposed to F7 with different fingering in the first two bars. In bars 33-34, I target the notes of an F Major triad throughout, and the violin harmonises the line using the same principle. The melody in bar thirty-five implies a C7b9 chord, the dominant (V) of F7.

Bars 37-40

This Brad Paisley-influenced line is formed from two bars of pedal steel-style bends followed by two bars of open strings featuring various doubled notes on different strings. Bar forty uses notes from the G Minor Pentatonic scale to add some contrast.

Bars 41-44

Although this passage features a 12-tone row, I have included asterisks here because it does use orthodox chromatic approach note concepts.

Bars 45-48

I use a mix of chromatic techniques in this Jerry Reed-style line. The beginning is another example of how bridging and approach note movements can be combined to form one elaborate five-note enclosure motif.

Bars 49-52

This section features Example 1b transposed to D7.

Bars 53-56

I play Example 2b again, this time transposed to F7. The start of this line begins as a straightforward ascending F Bebop scale run (although these are usually played descending rather than ascending). Once again, I briefly transition to the darker F Minor 6 Pentatonic in bar fifty-five before returning to F Mixolydian.

F Bebop Scale	F	G	A	Bb	C	D	Eb	E
Formula	1	2	3	4	5	6	b7	7

F Bebop scale Shape 1

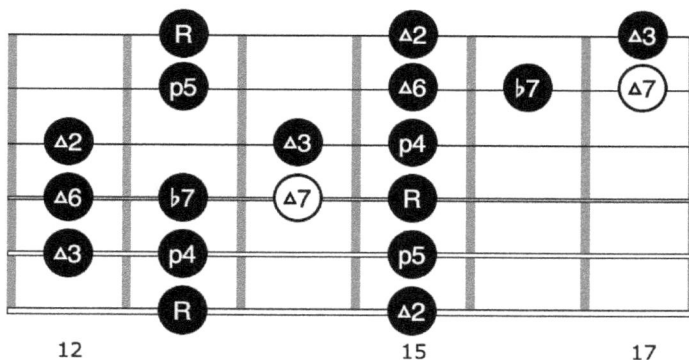

Bars 57-60

I add a bit of balance by avoiding chromatic notes, but create interest using open strings and three-against-four rhythmic groupings.

Bars 61-64

I play some more pedal steel-style bends here and once again the b3 and b5 passing notes highlight the interplay between Mixolydian and the Minor Blues scale.

Bars 65-68

The line here is Example 3n transposed to C7. It's highly chromatic, so be aware of what you are playing throughout.

Bars 69-72

I used hybrid picking in the Brent Mason-style line in bars 71-72 but you can use whatever's comfortable.

Bars 73-76

As in bars 21-24, this is a continuation of the chromatic theme – an identical four-note idea shifted down in whole steps that extends the tone row from 12 to 16 notes.

Bars 77-80

I finish by targeting notes of a G Major triad with the same enclosure motif on each string. This is mimicked a diatonic 3rd higher by the harmony guitar on the backing track.

MIXED CHROMATIC TECHNIQUES SOLO STUDY #2

[Each chromatic note is indicated with an asterisk]

(Shaun Baxter)

'Del. Res' = delayed resolution   'Enc.' = enclosure   'Br.' = bridging   'A.N.' = approach-note

113

8va
F7
Loco
33
34
35
36
A.N.
G7
37
38
39
40
Let ring
BU
PB10
LD
m
A7
41
42
43
44
Hold
12-tone row
C7
45
46
47
48
Ring
Br.
Enc.
Del. Res.

D7
8va
P.M. (slightly)
A.N.
F7
Br.
Fm6 pentatonic scale
1/4 (curl)
Enc.
Del. Res.
G7
(3)
Ring
A7
BU
Br.
A.N.
Ring
Enc.

C7
Br.
Br.
Enc.
Br.
Br.
A.N.
Del. Res.
D7
Br.
Enc.
Del. Res. or Enc.
F7
(4)
(4)
(4)
A.N.
Hold
BU
A.N.
Serialism
12-tone row
(w/harmony)
G7
(5)
(5)
(5)
(5)
(5)
A7
Enc.
Enc.
Enc.
Enc.
Enc.

Conclusion

I hope this book has helped to open up new vistas in your soloing, and that the principles you've learned will allow you to use *all* twelve notes rather than just those from a five- or seven-note scale.

Apart from expanding your tonality, chromaticism gives access to dissonance which, if used with taste, will help you introduce contrast between tense non-scale notes and settled scale notes. In other words, *tension* and *resolution* – an essential aspect of musical balance.

Although I have used the Mixolydian scale as a workhorse throughout this book, every chromatic principle can (and should) be applied to any other scale you know. Your immediate next steps should be to apply these ideas to Dorian, Aeolian and the Major scale, but bear in mind that often the best notes to target are chord tones.

My aim has been to offer you varied musical examples that comprise a balance of different musical elements and this is something to keep in mind when creating your own ideas. Aside from writing lines that are interesting and ear-catching, you should also ensure they are always expressive and musical.

Never lose sight of what makes good music and remember to have fun!

Shaun

www.ingramcontent.com/pod-product-compliance
Lightning Source LLC
Chambersburg PA
CBHW081428090426

42740CB00017B/3220